A COMPLETE CULINARY HERBAL

Reveals the healthful constituents of herbs; how they make food and drinks more appetizing, provide useful and visually enjoyable foliage, and yield their nostalgic scents in sachets and pot-pourris.

Oriental Poppy

A COMPLETE CULINARY HERBAL

A Guide to Growing, Drying and
Using Herbs as Flavours and Scents

AUDREY WYNNE HATFIELD

Illustrated by the author

NATURE'S WAY

THORSONS PUBLISHERS LIMITED
Wellingborough, Northamptonshire

First published as *Pleasures of Herbs* 1964
Second Impression 1966
Third Impression 1972
First published in *Nature's Way* series 1978

ISBN 0 7225 0442 X

Printed and bound in Great Britain by
Weatherby Woolnough, Wellingborough
Northamptonshire

For

"JOCK"—DR G. WILSON FORBES

and

DR PAUL STRICKLAND

Acknowledgements

SOME of the items in this book have been extended from my short features which appeared over a period of two years in the *Observer*, and I should like to thank the editor of that newspaper for allowing me to use them.

AUDREY WYNNE HATFIELD

Contents

		PAGE
ACKNOWLEDGEMENTS	. . . .	6
INTRODUCTION	. . . .	15

I. THE HERBS

ALECOST	. . . .	23
ALKANET	. . . .	25
ANGELICA	. . . .	27
ANISE	. . . .	29
ARTEMISIAS	. . . .	32
BALM	. . . .	35
BASIL	. . . .	38
BAY	. . . .	41
BERGAMOT	. . . .	43
BORAGE	. . . .	45
BURNET	. . . .	47
CARAWAY	. . . .	49
CLOVE CARNATION	. . . .	51
CHAMOMILE	. . . .	54
CHERVIL	. . . .	57
CHIVES	. . . .	59
COMFREY	. . . .	59
CORIANDER	. . . .	62
DANDELION	. . . .	64
DILL	. . . .	67
ELDER	. . . .	70
FENNEL	. . . .	73
GARLIC	. . . .	75
HYSSOP	. . . .	78
LAVENDER	. . . .	81
LOVAGE	. . . .	84
MARIGOLD	. . . .	86

		PAGE
MARJORAM	.	89
MINT	.	92
WATER CRESS AND NASTURTIUM	.	95
PARSLEY	.	98
POPPY	.	101
ROSE	.	104
ROSEMARY	.	107
RUE	.	110
SAGE	.	113
SAVORY	.	117
SORREL	.	119
SWEET CICELY	.	122
TANSY	.	126
TARRAGON	.	128
THYME	.	121
VIOLET	.	134

II. FLAVOURS—HERBS IN THE KITCHEN

APPETIZERS:

Rue Sandwiches	.	137
Canapés	.	137
Herb Cheese Canapés	.	137

BISCUITS:

Herb Biscuits	.	137
Mint Puff Biscuits	.	138
Rosemary and Tansy	.	138
Cheese Straws	.	138
Cheese Biscuits	.	138

BREAD:

With Herbs	.	138
Pulled Bread	.	139

BUTTERS:

Herb Butters	.	139
Chivry Butter	.	139
Maître d'Hôtel Butter	.	139
Green Butter	.	140
Montpelier Butter	.	140

PAGE

Ravigote Butter 140
Green Dye 140
Rose Petal Butter 140
Herb Butter for Beef Steaks 141
Water Cress Butter 141

CAKES:

Caraway Seed Cake 141
Poppy Cakes 141
Goosnargh Cakes 141
Lemon or Orange Cake with Coriander Seeds . . 142
Flannel Cakes 142

CHEESE:

Cheese of Seven Herbs 142
Milk Cheese 142
Savoury Flans or Savoury Cheese Cakes . . 143
Milk Cheese "Cream" 143

CONSERVES:

Lavender Conserve 143
Mint Conserve 144
Rose Conserve 144
Rosemary Conserve 144
Violet Conserve 144

DESSERT 144

DRINKS:

Angelica Liqueur 144
Elder-berry Syrup 145
Cups and Punches 145
Wines 145

EGG DISHES:

Scrambled Eggs 146
Baked Custard 146
Egg Custard Sauce 146
Savoury Pancakes 146
Royales 146
Seasoned Pudding 147
Poached Egg on Water Cress Purée . . . 147

PAGE

FISH:

Whitefish Steaks 147
A Simple Stuffing 147
Fish Fillets or Steaks 147
Curried Fish 147
The Most Suitable Herbs to accompany Fish . . . 148

FLOWERS:

Candied and Crystallized 148
Angelica 148
Rose Petals 149
Mint Leaves, Other Leaves, and Petals . . . 149
Posies and Sprays inside Jellies 150

FORCEMEAT:

For Turkey, Veal, Fowl and Game 150
Minty Stuffing or Forcemeat 150

FRITTERS:

Savoury Fritters 151
Sweet Fritters 151
Comfrey Fritters 151

GAME AND POULTRY:

Hare 152
Grouse and Pigeon 152
Chicken Boiled 152
Chicken Roasted 152
Duck 152
Goose 152
Partridge 152
Pheasant 152
Turkey 152

ICES 152

JAMS:

Rose-petal Jam 153
Angelica and Rhubarb Jam 153
Apple and Mint Jam 153
Elder-berry Jelly 153

JELLIES:

Mint Jelly 154
Parsley Jelly 154
Sage Jelly 154
Lavender Jelly 154
Jellies for Dessert 155
Lemon Jelly 155
Orange Jelly 155

MEAT:

Beef Roasted 155
Lamb, Mutton, and Beef Roasted 155
Beef Mince 156
Beef Stew 156
Beef Steak 156
Lamb Chops or Cutlets 156
Lamb Stew 156
Ham Roast or Boiled 156
Pork Chops 156
Pork Roasted 156
Veal Cutlets 156
Veal Roast 156
Rissoles 156
Sausages 156
Tripe 156

PASTRY 157

PICKLES:

Pickled Cucumber with Dill 157
Pickled Cucumbers with Dill and Fennel . . . 158
Dill and Collyflower Pickle 158
Nasturtium Seeds for Imitation Capers . . . 158
Pickled Elder Shoots like Indian Pickle . . . 158
Pickled Elder Shoots in Imitation of Indian Bamboo . . 159

PUDDINGS:

Rice Pudding and Cornflour Shape 159
Tansy Pancakes 159
Tansy Pudding of Ground Rice 160

PAGE

Mint Pasty 160
Elder-flowers 160
Elder-flower Pancakes 160
Elder-flower Milk 160

SALADS 161

SAUCES:

Savoury Sauces 163
Almond Sauce 164
Anisette Sauce 164
Béchamel Sauce with Herbs 164
Dill Sauce 164
Fennel and Parsley 164
Fennel Sauce 164
Tarragon Sauce 165
Parsley and Tarragon Sauce 165
Tomato Cream Sauce (American) 165
Tomato Sauce (Italian) 166
Sorrel Sauce 166

SEASONINGS:

Mustard 166
Continental Mustard 167
Herb Mustard 167
Mild Herb Mustard 167
Mustard with Dried Herbs 167
Herb Pepper 167
Herb Salt 167

SOUPS:

Herb Flavourings 168
"Chiffonade" Garnish 168
Water Cress Soup 168
Chervil Soup 169
Consommé à la Chiffonade 169
Chervil Potage 169
Herb Potage 170
Sorrel Soup 170

PAGE

TEAS:
    Herb Teas 170
VEGETABLES 172
VINEGARS: 174
    Herb Vinegars 174
    Mixed Herb Vinegar 174
    Garlic Vinegar 174
    Shallot Vinegar 174
    Tarragon Vinegar 174
    Elder-flower Vinegar 175
    Vinegars in Variety 175

III. SCENTS—TOILET USES

BATH SCENTS 176
ELDER-FLOWER WATER 176
FOOT-BATH 176
HAIR-DARKENER 176
HAIR-WASH 176
HERB PILLOWS 177
LAVENDER VINEGAR 177
ROSE VINEGAR 177
VIOLET VINEGAR 177
VIOLET, JASMINE AND ROSE VINEGAR 177
SWEET BAGS 177
SWEET WASHING WATERS 178
STINGS 178
TEETH 178
POT-POURRIS 178

IV. GROWING HERBS IN ANY GARDEN

MAKING A HERB GARDEN 181
TOWN HERB GARDENS 182
SUITABLE HERBS FOR TOWN GARDENS:
    Shrubby Permanents 183
    Herbaceous Perennials 183
    Biennial 183

PAGE

Annuals from Seed 183
Herbs for Window-boxes 183
Herbs for Pots or Indoor Window-sills 184
Drying Herbs for Winter Use 184
Drying Herbs for Home Use 185

SHORT BIBLIOGRAPHY 186

Introduction

THE term "Herb" rightly applies to any soft-stemmed plant, but it is now popularly used for those that are useful in cookery, or for their aromatic scent or medicinal value. Thus it includes woody-stemmed bushes like Rosemary, Lavender, Thyme, Sage, Winter Savory, Bay, etc. The serious use of plants in medicine is the province of herbalists and homoeopathic practitioners, who employ most species of herbage from mosses to trees, but this book is limited to the comparatively few "culinary herbs" which give most pleasure today, and are easy to grow or obtain either fresh or dried.

Much awareness of the edible and remedial qualities of all herbage must have been gained (by sad and happy experiences) in prehistoric days. When food was scarce and often nasty, the pungent herbs made it more palatable, and the larger, succulent-leaved ones provided salads and vegetables; many also would heal wounds and ease suffering, as even the tastiest "culinary herb" had its real medicinal virtues. Early civilizations inherited the knowledge and developed it, and both doctors and cooks used herbs appreciatively and with increasing effect. Doctors experimented with every kind of plant, cooks with the flavorous types.

Researches into plants' curative powers were early recorded, notably by Greek doctors: by Hippocrates in 460 B.C.; 200 years later by Theophrastus; then, about A.D. 60, Dioscorides compiled his *De Materia Medica*, which was the foundation of all medical treatment in western Europe until after the 16th century, when translations were made of the important works of Galen, a brilliant Greek physician who had lived from A.D. 130 to 200.

But the imagination is perhaps more generally and pleasurably stimulated by the recordings of the use of herbs as scents and flavourings; these give another dimension to history, its smells and the taste of its food. What delicious blendings of herbs, spices, flowers and wines went into the famous sauces of the elegant, luxury-loving Sybarites, who, over 2,000 years ago, publicly and handsomely rewarded any inventor of a new exquisite sauce? They slept on beds of fresh uncrumpled Rose petals in Sybaris, the most opulent city of Greater Greece. Tragically, for the Sybarites and posterity, their superb city was razed during a political war, and their Croton enemy, by diverting the river, drowned the ruins. Many of the flowers and herbs required for Sybaris, and elsewhere, were cultivated in the then fertile plains around Paestum or Posidonia, the daughter colony of Sybaris, and, happily, its ruins are still to be seen embedded in Roses and Violets.

The odour of herbs must have been characteristic of ancient Greece. It escaped from kitchens and shops, from trodden herbs strewn on pavements and in public halls, theatres, courts and temples; the smoke of burning herbs drifted from numerous altars, as did herb-scented steam from the public baths; the bathed citizens smelled of herbs, as certain kinds, according to their significance, were rubbed on bathers; Mint, the scent of strength, went on the arms, Thyme on the breast, as the smell of courage and all virtues (to "Smell of Thyme" was a popular term of high praise of virtue and style in Athens).

The Violet was the emblem of Athens, etched on pavements, worn as chaplets (as were Roses) to deter drunkenness. Violets were made into wine, salads and scents, and strewn on the floors of banqueting halls and temples. And Roses too were eaten, drunk, worn and enjoyed in every possible way. Grecian bees were pastured on acres of particular herbs to produce honey of various flavours which were famous. Food and wines were flavoured with such herbs as are used today.

Superstitious significance had long been attached to plants, and in classical mythology several kinds were dedicated to each deity. Prayers were carried to Olympus on the scented smoke of burning herbs (as for centuries they have been sent to heaven). At Delphi, Apollo's oracle, the priestess, was drugged to frenzy probably with Thorn Apple and the fumes from burning herbs in the pit below, when she uttered her predictions through teeth clenched on excitant Bay leaves, Apollo's particular herb.

The Romans too employed flowers and herbs in every possible way. Their baths and bathers were made fragrant with them (Lavender being the choice for the elegant who could afford its high price). Roses were imported by the shipload from Egypt to help satisfy the great demand for the petals. They were also grown in Italy where, to get the blooms out of season, vast nurseries were equipped with networks of heating pipes. Like the then vanished Sybarites, rich Romans fancied Rose-petal beds (especially marriage beds). For banquets, appetite-provoking Mint was rubbed on tables and trodden with other herbs and flowers strewn on floors. Rose garlands were the décor, Rose petals garnished certain dishes and made salad, and, as in Greece, in the belief that Roses prevented or delayed drunkenness, Rose chaplets were worn and Rose petals were dropped into wine-cups. Both Rose and Violet wines were popular. Many other flowers, particularly Clove Carnations, were lavishly used not only for decorations but in food and for wine-making. Such flower and herb wines may be better imagined when it is remembered that the principal ingredients of the liqueur Chartreuse are Carnations, Balm, Hyssop, Angelica and other herbs. And two delicious French liqueurs are made from Roses, "L'Huile de Rose," and "Parfait Amour," while Vermouth's appetizing flavour comes from Roman Wormwood (*Artemisia pontica*).

Many of today's uses of herbs in fine cookery originated in Roman kitchens. Roman cooks discovered the delicious excellence of Mint sauce and explored all the delectable herb flavours and scents. The rich Romans stuffed their mattresses and cushions with herbs, and the colonizers introduced the plants throughout the Empire. Every advantage was taken of the fertility of Britain, and by the Romans' skilful agricultural methods it was made to yield for export to Rome vast quantities of wheat and the produce of numerous orchards and herb gardens (humming with Italian bees). Some herbs grew better in the British climate than elsewhere and the honey was good.

The herb which coloured much of the past was Saffron, its musky-scented yellow powder being enjoyed by all, from the Far East to the Atlantic coast. Persian royal robes were dyed with it. Greek and Roman cities were golden with it on great occasions when Saffron water was sprinkled in public buildings, and the streets were powdered with it along processional routes. At all times food was often tinted and flavoured with Saffron. But the smell that was consistently breathed over the entire "Old World" from the most distant past into the future was Garlic, used as a subtle flavouring only by gourmets, but eaten in bulk by the less sensitive.

After the fall of Rome, during the Dark Ages, the subtleties of classical cookery languished, especially in Britain where the barbarous invading Saxons effectively wiped out Roman-British culture leaving the corpse-strewn towns and lovely Italian-style frescoed, mosaic-floored, central-heated villas to decay, and the orchards and herb gardens to revert to nature. Some plants survived to become naturalized, and it is even possible that our wild Cherry is descended from Roman trees. The Continentals fared better, and as time passed the Anglo-Saxons, becoming less rude and more travelled (for trade or pleasure), acquired the taste for French food and wines and other elegancies. They became great herb-fanciers and used as many as 500 plants in medicine and cookery, whilst a mere 380 were recorded as useful on the Continent. There was much trafficking in herbs and their uses. King Alfred swapped them with his foreign friends, and about A.D. 900 his confidant, Bald, had his famous Leech Book compiled, using much of Alfred's data.

Although many religious orders sternly forbade the practice of medicine, certain monasteries cultivated herbs in their hortyards or physic gardens and imported some from Continental monasteries. They used them with the ancient understanding of their curative and culinary worth and sold the surplus to the public to defray the cost of their gardens' maintenance. Until the 14th century these monastic establishments provided the only "hospitals," infirmaria, for the sick, and the only desirable inns for travellers in Britain. English visitors to the Continent reported inns there which not only served food and wine of un-home-like excellence, but provided scented pillows filled with herbs or Violets, also herb mouth-washes and Rose-water to wash the face. More and more of this foreign polish caught on at home as returning Crusaders, having tasted exotic foods and hobnobbed with fastidious strangers, brought more herbs, spices and flowers to medieval England, requiring their food enriched and their comforts refined. Meanwhile, ladies embroidered scarves for their knights and crusading lords with sprays of Thyme, still the symbol of courage, as it had been in ancient Greece. Saffron was re-introduced and became the fashionable hue; hair, faces and clothes became yellow as did food. Most dishes were sent to table powdered with Saffron.

The Frenchifying of English living was unquestionably further stimulated during the Hundred Years War with France, when in the early successful decades rich plunder was brought home along with French nobles. These captives often waited several years for their ransoms to be paid, and while staying as guests with their captors they charmed their households and refined their habits and cuisines.

The scent of herbs had always been appreciated, and clothes chests had long been fitted with special compartments to contain aromatic herbs to sweeten the garments and deter moths. Herbs with flowers and scented roots were placed in the best beds, and bunches of freshly gathered herbs and flowers were usual in bed-chambers, sitting-rooms and galleries. Henry III, in 1251, ordered the wall outside the royal bedroom at Guildford palace to be pulled down and re-built fifteen feet further away to permit a herb garden to be made between the bed-chamber and the wall. He also had the gutters of the White Tower of London extended to prevent rain dripping down and spoiling the whitened walls.

It is pleasant to remember that in the herb-conscious London of the Middle Ages, almost all the houses, churches and great buildings were whitewashed as a preservative, and that they were frequently gaily decorated, for religious and superstitious reasons, with garlands of herbs and flowers; Saints' days were very frequent and always enjoyably observed, and evil spirits had to be discouraged. There were many London gardens great and small, and the gardeners of the gentry and rich citizens sold herbs and other produce beside the gateway of St. Paul's Churchyard. Herb-women, crying their wares in the streets, hawked wild herbs from the countryside and others from the market gardens outside the city walls (the present Camomile Street, Bishops-gate, was probably one). To these plots were taken the loads of refuse dumped in the streets, the rich compost of garbage, stale floor-coverings of hay, straw, rushes, or, after special occasions, of strewing herbs and flowers.

The posies of aromatic herbs generally carried were held to the nose to mitigate the town's insanitary smells and as supposed disinfectants against disease. The custom still existing of carrying herb-posies into court during assizes originated from this supposition, as a protection against jail-fever (typhus) from which prisoners often suffered.

For feasting, tables and benches were rubbed with odorous herbs, food was flavoured with them, and floors were strewn with them, so that the herb-crowned diners when replete often fell from their seats and slept on them. Many years later Gerard, writing of Mint, said: "The smell rejoiceth the heart of man, for which cause they used to strew it in chambers and places of recreation, pleasure and repose, where feasts and banquets are made."

Jolly annual pilgrimage parties were enjoyed by many, usually to English shrines, but venturesome tourists made for the Continental ones, taking with them insect-deterring herbs and bringing back a greater taste for the foreigners' food and his uses of herbs, culinary, medicinal and superstitious.

In Tudor England the herb garden for domestic supplies was important to every housewife. Plants were needed for home-doctoring, and for the kitchen and still-room where toilet-waters, "sweete bags," syrups, ointments, cosmetics, herb-flavoured ale, wines, cordials, conserves, perfumes and scented candles were prepared, and an amazing number of herbs and flowers, roots and shoots were used. Food was generally cooked with herbs and served garnished with them, accompanied by elaborate herb sauces and salads. Fish, meats, game and poultry, with heron, swan, peacock and the newly introduced turkey from Mexico, all had their most fancied herb-flavoured stuffings. Herbs too were the flavourings for many puddings, dessert and sweetmeats, and there were wonderfully contrived bouquets of herbs, flowers and fruits imprisoned in jellies.

Sea-going adventurers brought novel plants from abroad to English gardens. "It is a world also to see how many strange herbs, plants, and annual fruits are daily brought unto us from the Indies, Americas, Taprobane (Ceylon), Canary Isles, and all parts of the world," said the reverend William Harrison (about 1587). He claimed to grow 300 uncommon plants in his "300 foot of ground" and extolled the glories of "Hampton Court, Nonsuch, Tibault's, Cobham Garden." John Gerard, who wrote one of the best known "herbals," had his famous garden in Holborn near the Fleet river, where he grew over 1,000 species of plants.

French cooking continued in favour, and according to Harrison most of the cooks employed by the nobility of England were "musical-headed Frenchmen and strangers" who, from surviving recipes and garden lists, made full use of herbs. In the 17th century Virginia was finally colonized and the settlers took their familiar European herbs to the New World. And in 1656 Europe was enriched by the introduction of the American aromatic plant, "Bergamot," which was a new scent and a novel flavour. The apothecaries' shops were stocked with all manner of herbs and herbal commodities. Of Mint alone there was the dried and fresh herb, mint water, spirits of mints, syrup of mints, conserve of the leaves, the simple oil and "chimical oyle."

At this time the method of extracting the pure and lasting scent of Rose oil, the Otto or Attar, was discovered by a happy accident. For the wedding festivities of a Persian princess a wide ditch was dug around the palace gardens and filled with Rose-water. The wedded couple, whilst rowing on this fragrant canal, noticed the heat of the sun separating the oil from the water, and on skimming it off they found it exquisitely perfumed. The possibilities of the process were recognized and manufacture of this perfume began immediately. It was to pervade fashionable assemblies for many generations and became the basis of all Rose scents.

Ever since the early days of printing, beautiful "Herbals" had appeared describing plants and stressing their medicinal (and superstitious) virtues. Several physic gardens were now established, the forerunners of botanic gardens, and after Charles II granted its charter to the Royal Society of London in 1662 both the sciences of medicine and of botany rapidly progressed, very closely allied. It is interesting to note how many of culinary herbs' constituents still remain in medical formulas.

The regular use of a large variety of culinary herbs and flowers continued until the end of the 19th century. The Victorians employed them almost as assiduously as the ancients had done. But in this 20th century many pleasurable herbs and their possibilities have been neglected and their popular usage has become unimaginatively limited. Fortunately, there is now a revival of interest and appreciation of such herbs as are used on the Continent, and people with gardens are realizing the beauty of herb plants and the added pleasure of growing them to use freshly picked. People living in flats are raising the accommodating kinds in pots on window-sills, and planting them in window-boxes. In town gardens they are grown in boxes, tubs and large pots on balconies and in back yards. Certain modern nurseries are devoted to herb culture, and reputable firms carefully dry and package them. Now all the delicious old favourite herb flavours are available fresh or dried, and many of the old recipes which used them should be tried and again enjoyed.

I. The Herbs

ALECOST

Alecost, Costmary, either name is used for this attractive old herb, which is still seen in some Lincolnshire village gardens. It is called there Sage O' Bedlem, or Bethlehem, from the Sage-like shape of the leaves and its ancient dedication to the Virgin Mary. It is Our Lady's Mint; in France, Herbe Sainte-Marie. Sometimes it is called Mace for its aromatic spicy taste. Because of the shape of the notched leaves, it is known as Goose Tongue.

Alecost is seldom seen today but it used to be in most gardens, and it is worth growing not only as a good foliage plant to contrast with other things, but for its several pleasant uses. It reaches three feet high, is lush and cool-looking, and its long broad leaves of pale green have a subtle balsamic scent. It is of the Daisy family, Compositae, and the loose clusters of flowers appearing in August are like insignificant rayless Daisies. This herb is a native of Asia and was probably brought to Britain by the Romans who valued its medicinal properties, also its scent and flavour.

In Green's *Universal Herbal* (1532), a strong infusion of Costmary leaves is said to be "good in disorders of the stomach and head" and in the same century Lyte reported Costmary was common in all gardens; Gerard said: "It groweth everywhere in gardens," and it was described by Parkinson among the sweet herbs in his garden. The latter said: "The conserve made with leaves of Costmaria and sugar doth warm and dry the brain and openeth the stoppings of the same; stoppeth all catarrhes, rheums and distillations, taken in the quantitie of a beane." Culpepper, too, prescribed this herb and said: "It is an especial friend and help to evil, weak and cold livers." Costmary was also popular for making "Sweete washing water," "Sweete bags" and for mixing in pot-pourri.

Alecost is properly called *Tanacetum balsamita*, the specific name refers to its balsam-like odour. Its leaves were once used to give their

Alecost

spicy flavour to ale, hence the name Alecost; Costmary came from the Latin *costum*, an oriental plant.

Costmary leaves have a minty taste that is pleasantly bitter, they are chopped up in salads and in veal stuffing and forcemeat. The plant is a hardy perennial and easy to grow in light rich soil in a sunny position. Its roots quickly spread, and it may have to be divided every few years.

ALKANET

One obvious reason for planting Alkanets in a 20th-century herb or flower garden is for the sake of their amazing display of brilliant flowers, especially those of *Anchusa italica*, the best known Alkanet. This five-foot-tall perennial with hairy leaves and branching stems alight with blossoms had an interesting past. The name was said to be derived from the Greek *anchousa*, a paint or dye, because the roots' rind produced a red dye which was used as a cosmetic for colouring the cheeks and lips of the ancient Egyptians, Greeks and Romans. In the 17th century, Parkinson said that French ladies coloured their faces with an ointment of Alkanet, but the tint was fleeting.

The Greek physician Dioscorides not only advised Alkanet for relieving several ailments but stressed its efficacy for curing serpent bites, and went further, saying: "If any that have newly eaten it do spit into the mouth of a serpent, the serpent instantly dies." Culpepper, too, had faith in its healing powers for such complaints as jaundice, ulcers and gravel, and said: "It is an herb of Venus and indeed one of her darlings."

Another desirable Alkanet is the evergreen type, *A. sempervirens*, about two feet high, that is sometimes found naturalized as a garden escape, often near old abbeys. The name Alkanet is a corruption of *alcana*, from the Arabic *al-henna*, the henna plant, which was used to dye finger- and toe-nails, hair and heels; it probably arose from Alkanet's similar uses.

Alkanet dye is also used to stain marble flesh-pink, to colour the liquid in the huge ornamental bottles in chemists' shops, also for staining wood and the lower grades of port wine. The edible flowers are a charming and ancient decoration for salads and other dishes and are good for candying.

Alkanets belong to the Boraginaceae family, so they frequently produce both blue and pink flowers together. They are easy to grow, but

Alkanet

Anchusa italica sometimes succumbs to hard winters and needs to be renewed quite often. It generally produces many useful seedlings.

ANGELICA

Garden Angelica, the noble giant among true medicinal and culinary herbs, was the benevolent one, the comforter of man's distresses and some called it "The Root of the Holy Ghost." It probably originated in Syria, but travelled for so long and so far that it became naturalized throughout the cooler parts of northern Europe as far as Iceland and Lapland, where it was chewed to prolong life.

Its reputation as a medicinal plant was rooted in prehistoric times and was inevitably linked with superstitious, pagan beliefs which, persisting in early Christian minds, became associated with their spring-time festival of the Annunciation. The plant's name, *Angelica archangelica*, was supposed to have arisen from a vision in which an Archangel said it would cure the plague. As a further right to the name Angelica bloomed on the day of Michael the Archangel, which used to be 8th May. With such connections the plant was esteemed as an infallible guard against witches and evil spirits, able to frustrate their spells and enchantments, and it was deemed a complete protection against the contagion of infectious diseases. Angelica was man's remedy for almost any malady or grief.

An extraordinary survival of the pagan belief in Angelica was the custom kept alive in the area now a part of Latvia. In the lake districts where the plants were plentiful, annual processions of countrypeople carrying Angelica flower-stems to sell in the towns chanted a chorus so ancient that none of them understood its words or meaning, the early summer-time ritual having been handed down from generation to generation.

Angelica's many qualities were praised by the old writers, Gerard among them. He also said: "It cureth the bitings of mad dogs and all venomous beasts." The astrology-conscious Culpepper's great faith in this herb's curative powers covered as extensive a range as any, and he placed it as a herb of the Sun in Leo and advised its gathering. "When he is there, the Moon applying to his good aspect; let it be gathered either in his hour, or in the hour of Jupiter, let Sol be angular. Observe the like in gathering the herbs of other plants, and you may happen to do wonders." Parkinson, Apothecary to James I, in his beautiful book

Angelica

Paradise in Sole (1629), held Angelica to be about the most effective of medicinal herbs.

Angelica was grown everywhere and valued for all kinds of uses, and it can still be seen surviving, self-sown, in some of the London squares.

The whole plant from root to seed has a pleasant aromatic fragrance and flavour, and all parts are useful for various purposes. The roots yield a resinous gum which is often employed in perfumery as a substitute for musk benzoin; and it is suspected that in some Rhine wines the delicious flavour of muscatel grapes is due to the secret use of Angelica. It is one of the herbal ingredients of such liqueurs as the true French Absinthe in which the root is blended with Wormwood and other herbs. Both seeds and root go into Chartreuse; it partners Caraway seeds in the mixing of Kummel; the seeds help to flavour Vermouth and Gin; and the dried leaves are used in the preparation of bitters.

Some of Angelica's domestic uses include the boiling, like celery, of the tender mid-ribs of the leaves. In Lapland they consider the stalks a great delicacy, and in Iceland both roots and stems are eaten raw with butter. The young stems baked in hot ashes are relished in Finland, where they also like the healthful stimulating tea infused from the dried or fresh leaves, tasting rather like china tea. The Norwegians make a bread of the roots, and confectioners everywhere use Angelica's candied stems and seeds; in some Continental countries these are often put into cakes and comfits.

The splendid Angelica is not difficult to grow. It prefers a little shade and the tenderest leaf-stalks are produced when it is grown in a good deep soil containing plenty of humus. Where they are well placed they sometimes grow into enormous plants reaching eight feet tall, with huge leaves and round umbels of fragrant yellowish-green flowers. Angelica belongs to the Umbelliferae family, it is a biennial and dies after producing seeds. However, if the flowering-stems are cut down before they mature, the plant continues to grow for several summers, and it generally needs three or four years to reach its vast proportions.

ANISE

Our traditional custom of using special wedding cakes probably started with the Anise cakes called *mustacae*, with which the ancient

Romans finished a good rich meal. These cakes were made with a flour dough and spiced with Anise, Cummin and other aromatic seeds and they were generally served as the traditional finish to their wedding feasts. The mustacae were intended to prevent indigestion and wind, a service for which Anise continued to be valued, and many centuries later, Gerard said: "Aniseed helpeth the yoexing (belching) and hicket (hiccough)." Anise seed, like all aromatics, was of sufficient value in Roman times to be demanded as tax payments to which Jesus referred: "Woe unto you, scribes and Pharisees, hypocrites! for ye pay tithe of Mint and Anise and Cummin, and have omitted the weightier matters of the law."

As a native of Egypt, Greece, Crete and Asia Minor, Anise was well known and generally used; it was distributed over much of the Old World. The Egyptians cultivated it in quantity for their numerous uses of the leaves and the seeds in food, drink and medicines. The Greeks used it both as a spicy condiment for seasoning, and they also recognized its medicinal qualities which were enumerated by their physician Dioscorides. Pliny the Roman mentioned its curative virtues that were appreciated and exploited by his countrymen. The Romans planted large cultivation grounds in Tuscany for their supplies of Anise seed for flavouring food, mixing medicines and perfumes. And being a benevolent herb, Anise acquired a widespread superstitious reputation as a powerful averter of the evil eye.

The herb was used in Britain in the 14th century as a perfume, a flavouring and medicine, and was much liked as a condiment ground like pepper. It was grown first in monastic gardens, but many of the seeds were imported by the monks from foreign monasteries in more favourable climates. The plants were introduced into ordinary English gardens in the 16th century, and Turner in his herbal (1551) said: "Anyse maketh the breth sweter and swageth payne." From an early date Anise had a high medicinal reputation for relieving hard stubborn coughs, flatulence and colic. And it was extremely popular for catching mice who could not resist its scent when smeared on traps. In Langham's *Garden of Health* 1683, Anise was recommended as a reliever of dropsy; his recipe for the treatment said: "Fill an old cock with Polipody and Aniseeds, and seethe him well, and drinke the broth."

In France, Spain, Italy and South America, Anise is an important ingredient in the making and the flavouring of cordial liqueurs, the delicious Anisette being perhaps the best known.

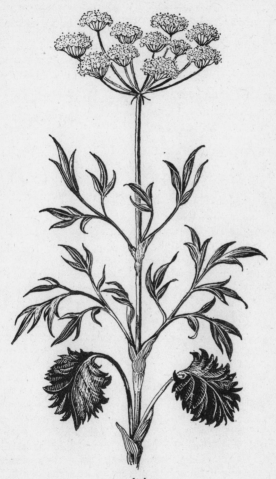

Anise

Anise is a more familiar herb and therefore more popular on the Continent than it is in Britain; it is used there to flavour bread and cakes and is put into soups, stews and other dishes and in confectionery. The finely-chopped leaves used discriminately give an unusual aromatic taste to salads, and in France they are often sprinkled as a garnish over a dish of young carrots. The powdered seeds are an ingredient of scent sachets and toilet preparations especially of certain tooth-pastes.

Anise is a charming annual, growing about eighteen inches to two feet high, with secondary feathery leaflets of bright green; from these it was given its generic name *Pimpinella*, from bipennella, meaning twice-pinnate, a medieval suggestion of the leaf-form. It is of the Umbelliferae group, and bears its white flowers in umbels like little umbrellas. The round aromatic fruits, the "seeds," do not always ripen in cool districts if the summer is wet and cold so that it is not a commercial crop in Britain. The best seeds are Spanish and known as Alicante Anise.

Apart from its pleasurable culinary uses, Anise is a very decorative foliage plant for the herb garden. The seeds can be sown outside in April in a warm sheltered situation, in a bed of dryish light soil. The flowers appear in early summer and are followed by the "seeds," which ripen in late summer or early autumn. Then the flower-stems may be cut at ground level and laid on sheets of clean paper in a warm room until they are completely dry, when they should be carefully shaken free of all bits of unwanted stuff.

Anise leaves have an antiseptic quality and make a good tisane for indigestion and a safe remedy for relieving acidity. The tea taken hot is excellent for colds.

ARTEMISIAS

Lad's Love, Boy's Love, Appleringie, Old Man, Southernwood, are old names for this ancient aromatic shrubby herb. It is one of the Wormwoods and its grey-green finely-cut foliage has the strong scent and bitterish lime or lemony taste associated with them. Southernwood is worth growing for the pleasure of picking the leaves in passing and pinching out their fragrance, which is generally pleasing to man but so highly distasteful to moths that the French call it "Garderobe" for its long service in protecting clothes.

The name Lad's Love survives from an old custom of making an

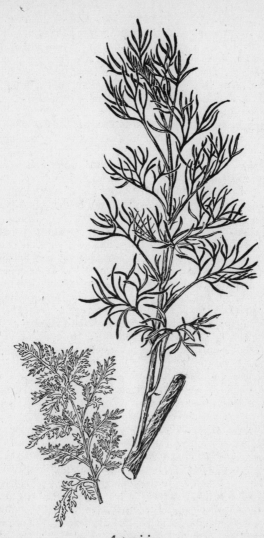

Artemisias

ointment with the ashes of the leaves to apply to a lad's face and induce an early beard. Also, a spray of leaves was traditionally included in the love bouquets presented by country lovers to their lasses, a Wormwood amongst flowers. This ancient custom was referred to in the 16th century by St. Francis de Sales: "To love in the midst of sweets, little children could do that, but to love in the bitterness of Wormwood is a sure sign of our affectionate fidelity."

The Greeks used this herb medicinally as reported by Dioscorides, for cramps, convulsions and other distresses. For the Romans, according to Pliny, it was an aphrodisiac among its other useful qualities. Gerard, too, upheld Pliny's opinions. In the days when fleas abounded, Southernwood was an effective strewing herb.

Lad's Love was grown in English gardens in Elizabeth I's time, and it was the custom to carry bunches of it with Balm to church, as their refreshing scent warded off drowsiness during the long sermons. In the belief that it was a potent disinfectant against contagion, it was one of the herbs placed beside prisoners in the dock to prevent their infecting the court with jail-fever. Among Culpepper's many uses for this herb he included some useful homely ones: "It taketh away inflammation of the eyes, if it be put with some part of wasted quince or boiled in a few crumbs of bread, and applied. Boiled in barley meal it taketh away pimples or wheals that rise in the face or other parts of the body . . . The herb bruised and laid to, helpeth to draw forth splinters and thorns out of the flesh . . . The ashes mingled with old salad oil, helpeth those that have their hair fallen, and are bald, causing the hair to grow again on the head or beard."

Southernwood is called *Artemisia abrotanum*, and it grows wild in Southern Europe. It is a hardy deciduous shrub growing about four feet tall. It is leggy and sprawling unless clipped back in March. Hedges of Southernwood are attractive and easy to train.

Old Woman, *Artemisia absinthium*, the Common Wormwood, the Green Ginger of gardens, is a lovely perennial about three feet high, with silvery lace-like foliage when grown in dryish soil, if too richly fed the silver turns green. This type is very hardy and grows wild from Siberia through Europe to America. Mexican women wear chaplets of it at their festival of the Goddess of Salt. It was esteemed medicinally in ancient times and was famous for its effects when put into wine. The Egyptians dedicated it to Isis and carried it in their religious processions. The Romans piled it on their altars at the *Latinae* festival, and they gave a drink made from it to the victors of their games and chariot races, to give them health and longevity. Pliny said the draught was the most ancient of herbal drinks. The French liqueur Absinthe was made from this Wormwood.

Old Warrior, Roman Wormwood, *Artemisia pontica*, is another decorative Wormwood and a native of Southern Europe. It also has the characteristic finely-cut leaves silvered with fine white hairs. It reaches about two feet high, and has a strong aromatic scent and the bitterish flavour of Wormwoods. This one is used in the making of the liqueur Vermouth, and has medicinal uses. Old Warrior is not quite so hardy as the two other types but given a sheltered position it should be safe in ordinary winters. It is a good plant for a cold greenhouse.

The Artemisias were dedicated to the Greek goddess Artemis, Diana of the Romans. There are a number of species in the group which belongs to the Compositae family, and they bear daisy-like flowers. But the plants are desirable for their lovely foliage which is useful dried for pot-pourris and for placing among clothes and furs. A few sprigs are sometimes liked in salads, and a tisane of Wormwood is helpful to relieve melancholia and to take the yellow from the skins of jaundice patients.

BALM

"Balm is sovereign for the brain, strengthening the memory and powerfully chasing away melancholy," wrote John Evelyn. "Let a syrup made with the juice of it and sugar be kept in every gentlewoman's house, to relieve the weak stomachs and sick bodies of their poor, sickly neighbours," instructed Culpepper. Lemon Balm is often confused with the tender Lemon Verbena, but it is a stauncher plant, hardy and faithful and will grow in the most unexpected places. The branching stems are about three feet high, and bear heart-shaped, toothed leaves which emit a lemony fragrance when touched and are lemon flavoured when tasted. The small white flowers appear in bunches from the leaf-axils. Balm, like most aromatic plants, has a balsamic oil content that is scientifically recognized as effective for dressing open wounds, and it was for this virtue that Dioscorides and other ancient physicians advised Balm to close up wounds without "peril of inflammation." Pliny too extolled this herb's healing powers, saying: "It is of so great virtue that though it be but tied to his sword that giveth the wound, it stauncheth the blood."

Gerard agreed, and said: "The juice of Balm glueth together greene wounds."

The famous Swiss physician Paracelsus, who had revolutionary ideas of medicine in the 16th century, believed Balm would completely restore a man to new life, and this same belief was recorded in the *London Dispensary* (1696), which said, "An essence of Balm, given in Canary wine, every morning will renew youth, strengthen the brain, relieve languishing nature and prevent baldness." An earlier edition had maintained that "Bawme" was a cure for the bites of mad dogs, King's Evil and wrynecks among other disasters. All the old authorities agreed on Balm's cheering virtues, and in fact it actually has a tonic effect on the digestion and circulation.

In favour of Balm's wonderful powers, it has been put on record that Llewelyn, a prince of Glamorgan, who lived to be 108, always breakfasted on herb teas containing a preponderance of Balm. And that a certain John Hussey, of Sydenham, who survived 116 years, breakfasted daily, for fifty of them, on Balm tea sweetened with honey. It was a great soother of nerves and releaser of tensions.

Balm was popularly called "Bee Balm" because of its attractiveness to bees. It was the *apiastrum* of the Romans, who were in the habit of placing sprays of the herb in their hives to attract swarms. Pliny affirmed that when bees strayed away they found their way home by it. Gerard assured his readers that "It is profitably planted where bees are kept. The hives of bees being rubbed with the leaves of Bawme, causeth the bees to keep together, and causeth others to come with them."

This perennial herb was given its proper name *Melissa*, the Greek word for a bee, because of its association with them and with honey. It has square stems like all members of the Labiatae family to which it belongs, and which includes many of the most useful aromatic herbs. It is naturally at home in southern Europe, but was grown in Britain at a very early date and was probably brought here by the Romans. It is often found naturalized in the south of England, nearly always where it has survived long after the disappearance of the dwelling and its garden, where it was once grown for its many homely uses. Balm wine was a good country tipple, and Balm tea made from the fresh leaves was a favourite brew.

Melissa officinalis, to give Balm its proper name, contains a potent salt and a cordial oil which make it a pleasant, cooling and refreshing tisane. Both Balm and Borage are used in the mixing of Claret Cup, and

Balm

most cups will be improved by sprays of these herbs. Balm is the main ingredient of the famous Carmelite water that is still made in France and has the reputation of conferring long life, and of relieving nervous headaches and neuralgia.

Balm leaves are a good flavouring for soups and stews, and are liked finely chopped in salads. In Belgium and Holland, Balm leaves are employed in preparing their delicious pickled herrings and eels. They may be used to give a lemon flavour to stuffings, and are often mixed in pot-pourri.

Balm is not fussy about soil or position, but the plants grown in fairly rich soil are the most luxuriant. It may be grown from seed or root-cuttings, and it can be divided in spring or autumn.

BASIL

"The smell thereof is so excellent that it is fit for a king's house," said Parkinson of Sweet Basil. He shared with many ancient writers a curious fancy about Basil's supposed affinity with scorpions and said: "It is also observed that scorpions doe much rest and abide under these pots and vessells wherein Basil is planted." The old superstition held that a sprig of Basil laid under a pot would breed a scorpion, and when Basil was closely smelled it could cause a scorpion to arise in the brain. Culpepper, harassed by the ancient conflicting reports, said: "Galen and Dioscorides hold it is not fitting to be taken inwardly and Chrysippus rails at it. Pliny and the Arabians defend it. Something is the matter, this herb and rue will not grow together, no, nor near one another, and we know rue is as great an enemy to poison as any that grows." He quoted further fanciful evidence: "Mizaldus affirms, that being laid to rot in horsedung, it will breed venomous beasts. Hilarius, a French physician, affirms upon his knowledge, that an acquaintance of his, by common smelling to it, had a scorpion breed in his brain." No herb could have had so diverse a reputation as Basil, suspected by some and extolled by others.

Parkinson, reporting the use of Bush Basil early in the 17th century, said: "The ordinary Basill is in a manner wholly spent to make Sweete or washing waters among other sweet herbs, yet sometimes it is put into nosegays. The Physicall properties are to procure a cheerfull and merry hearte whereunto the seeds is chiefly used in powder." But on the Continent Basil was not only used as a pleasurable scent, but was among the most popular of culinary herbs and also had its place in

Basil

medicine. One curious use recorded by Dodoens, the Belgian herbalist, was that some people believed that: "A woman in labour, if she but hold in her hand a root of this herb together with the feather of a swallow shall be delivered without pain."

In parts of Roumania this herb by long tradition was reputed to bring such sympathy between people that any youth would love a maid from whose hand he accepted a sprig of Basil. In Italy, too, it was a love-token, and it symbolized "love washed with tears" in Crete. In Persia and Malaysia grief-stricken relatives planted Basil on their loved ones' graves, as the Egyptians strewed the flowers on those of their relatives.

But to the ancient Greeks Basil represented hatred and misfortune, they illustrated poverty as a sad woman in ragged clothes with Basil at her side. They believed the herb would not grow unless sown with curses and abuse. The Romans also believed Basil required to be reviled to flourish. It was valued in ancient times mainly as a scent and strewing herb.

Presenting little pots of Basil as a compliment was a Tudor custom, for the herb was loved for its clove-like perfume and Bush Basil was often grown as a pot plant on window-sills.

Basil is an Indian plant sacred to both Vishnu and Krishna; it is cared for in every Hindu home for its disinfecting virtues to cleanse the air and to protect the family from evil. A Basil leaf is placed on the breast of every dead Hindu as his passport to Paradise.

Basil was first grown in English gardens in the 16th century, when it became a favourite kitchen herb. Then it provided the especial flavouring of the Fetter Lane sausages which became famous in the 17th century. The name Basil is said to have derived from *basilikos*, royal, probably because it was used to make royal unguents, perfumes and medicines (some say the Plantagenets smelled of Basil). The generic name *Ocymum* refers to the fragrant leaves from the Greek, *ozo*, smell. *O. basilicum*, is the Sweet Basil (about two feet tall), and *O. minimum*, small, or least, is the Bush Basil (only six inches high). These valuable pot herbs are of the Labiatae family and are free from any harmful secretions. They are employed medicinally for fevers and upsets of the bladder and kidneys, and as flavouring for soups (especially turtle soup), rich stews, sausages and sauces.

The tender Basils must be treated as annuals. Plants from seed sown under glass in March may be planted out in June, or seeds may be sown outside in May in a sunny sheltered bed of rich soil.

BAY

"Neither witch nor devil, nor thunder or lightning will hurt a man in a place where a Bay Tree is," said Culpepper. And apart from these virtues, the Sweet Bay, Roman Laurel, *Laurus nobilis,* is a beautiful small tree with dark, glossy, aromatic evergreen leaves that have enriched both food and gardens, and given medicinal comfort for many centuries. Describing how much Bay meant to his countrymen in Tudor times, Parkinson said: "They serve both for pleasure and profit, both for ornament and use, both for honest civil uses and for physic, yea both for the sick and for the sound, both for the living and the dead." And more from this great plant-lover: "It serveth to adorn the house of God, as well as of man; to procure warmth, comfort, and strength to the limmes of men and women by bathings and anoyntings out and by drinks . . . inward: To season the vessels wherein are preserved our meates, as well as our drinkes; to crown or encircle as with a garland the heads of the living, and to sticke and decke forth the bodies of the dead; so that from the cradle to the grave we have still use of, we have still need of it."

In Culpepper's account of Bay's uses, superstitious and curative, he assigned it to the sun, under the sign of Leo, and said: "It resisteth witchcraft very potently, as also all the evils old Saturn can do to the body of man, and they are not a few." Quoting the Greek physician, he wrote: "Galen saith that the leaves or bark do dry and heal very much, and the berries more than the leaves. The bark of the root is less sharp hot, but more bitter, and hath some restriction withal, whereby it is effectual to break the stone, and good to open obstructions of the liver." He also advised Bay for the pestilence and other infectious diseases, rheumatic complaints, palsies, cramp, tremblings and "weariness and pains by sore travelling." A welcome relief for the long-distance traveller of Culpepper's day.

Sprays of Bay and Rosemary were usually carried at funerals, weddings and on any occasion that needed their protective blessings. If a Bay tree died it was considered an awful omen of death and disaster. Shakespeare referred to this belief in his play Richard II: "'Tis thought the King is dead: we will not stay, the Bay trees in our country are all wither'd."

The Noble Laurel's natural home was the Mediterranean regions where it grew up to sixty feet high. The beauty of its growth, its aromatic

Bay

leaves, the tiny yellowish flowers and its berries, the silky olive green or reddish bark, all impressed the ancient Greeks as being worthy of a god. They dedicated it to Apollo and assumed its mythological origin as the metamorphosis of the nymph Daphne, who, desired and pursued by the god, fled from his advances and was changed into this tree. As Apollo's plant, Bay was regarded as the emblem of the Sun God's powers, of protection against evil, of guarding man's social well-being, of conferring the gifts of culture, music, song and poetry, and of prophecy. As Apollo's symbol, crowns of Bay were presented to be worn by victors, heroes and those who were especially commended in the arts. At Delphi, the oracle of Apollo, the priestesses were probably first drugged to frenzy with stramonium, the Thorn Apple's product, then with the excitant and narcotic properties of Bay, when, with Bay leaves between their lips, they gave their fateful prophecies.

The wholesome aromatic Bay was used from earliest times as the favourite of food flavourings. It was equally fancied in savoury or sweet dishes. Soups, stews, roasts, meat, fish, puddings and custards were all enhanced with Bay leaves. And with Rosemary, they were the traditional garnish of almost any dish sent to table, including the famous English brawn, once a useful export.

The Bay Tree, *Laurus nobilis*, of the *Lauraceae* family, is the only true Laurel: the Common Laurel of gardens and parks is, in fact, of the Cherry tribe. *Laurus* was the old Latin name for the Bay.

Sweet Bay will grow in some shade, but it must have protection from winter's cold bitter winds. It requires a well-drained bed of good soil that is mixed with compost.

BERGAMOT

In 1656 English gardens were enriched by the introduction of the American swamp plant, the ornamental Bergamot, Bee Balm, Oswego Tea. All these popular names refer to some of its qualities; its scent is supposed to be reminiscent of the Bergamot Orange; bees love its plentiful nectar; a fragrant tea brewed from it was common in the United States (probably first made by the American Indians); it was found in large quantities in the damp land of Oswego, around Lake Ontario.

The plant's proper name, *Monarda didyma*, is commemorative of N. Monárdez, a Spanish botanist, who could have no better compliment.

Bergamot

It is among the most spectacular of herbs, and all the plant is strongly aromatic, from the young shoots to the large crimson flower-heads. These are trumpet-shaped, resembling those of Honeysuckle. As the scent is retained when dry, the leaves and flowers are a valuable ingredient of pot-pourris.

There are several modern garden forms available with flowers varying in colour from crimson to pale pink, but the crimson or the scarlet-flowered original is the most fragrant and desirable for flavouring tea, for decorating salads, and for drying.

Monarda is a perennial and likes a moist, lightish soil with plenty of humus in it. The flowers last longer when they have some shade from the afternoon sun than if they are exposed to full sunshine. In good rich ground, the plant often exceeds its normal height of two and a half feet, and it spreads more rapidly by its creeping roots rather as the Mints, to which it is related, being of the Labiatae family. It must be firmly planted with the runners buried; they work their own way to the surface as the roots become established. Root cuttings are easily taken in late spring and start well in a shady corner.

BORAGE

Writing of Borage, Gerard said: "The leaves and floures of Borage put into wine make men and women glad and merry and drive away all sadness, dullness and melancholy, as Dioscorides and Pliny affirme." Putting sprays of Borage into wine-cups is an old idea from ancient Greece and Rome and was surely based on the qualities of the plant's constituents; these actually cool drinks and have a wholesome and invigorating effect.

Borage is a beautiful plant with silvery-white, stiff hairs covering stem, leaf and calyx, producing a shimmering effect and a dazzling setting for the bright blue star-shaped flowers with their rich black cones of anthers. Often there are pink buds and flowers borne among the blue ones. This ability to produce simultaneously flowers of two colours is a characteristic of plants of the Borage family, Boraginaceae, of which the Forget-me-not is another example. Borage originated as a wild plant in Aleppo, but it has become naturalized in most parts of Europe. It escaped from gardens where it was grown and prized for its excellent qualities. Its cucumberish flavour made it a favourite salad-herb, and the young leaves and shoots were boiled as a pot-herb. The

Borage

flowers were always popular for decorating salads and other dishes, and were candied for pretty side-dishes.

The medicinal uses of Borage appear in almost every old herbal and book of plants. Greek physicians recommended it for a number of illnesses, and maintained that when steeped in wine it brought absolute forgetfulness. The diarist John Evelyn said it revived the hypochondriac and cheered the hard student. Parkinson advised it for expelling "pensiveness and melancholy," and Nicholas Culpepper prescribed Borage for putrid and pestilential fever, jaundice, rheumatism and other ailments. It was generally acclaimed as a cooling and soothing herb and particularly efficacious for kidney and pulmonary complaints.

The derivation of the plant's botanical name, *Borago*, is uncertain, but is probably from the Latin, *borra* or *burra*, rough hair. Linnaeus held it to be a corruption of *corago* (Latin *cor*, the heart, *ago*, to act) from its medicinal use as a heart sedative.

Borage is a hardy annual two feet tall and flourishes in any good soil. Plants will flower in June from seeds sown in spring, and when established in a garden, Borage sows its own seeds and becomes a permanent pleasure; any unwanted seedlings can be used in salads.

BURNET

Turner in his *Newe Herball*, 1551, describing Salad Burnet, said: "It has two little lieves like unto the wings of birdes, standing out as the bird setteth her wings out when she intendeth to flye. Ye Dutchmen call it Hergottes berdlen, that is God's little berde, because of the colour that it hath on topp." This refers to the crimson-tufted stigmas.

The cucumbery Salad Burnet was an old inhabitant of herb gardens; Parkinson listed it as grown in his famous London garden, and it was taken to America by the early settlers. It was the "Pimpernella" indispensable to the making of the best Italian and French salads. And from ancient times it was used like Borage to cool tankards and cups. Its generic name *Poterium* came from the Greek *poterion*, a drinking-cup, from the classic use of the leaves in preparing beverages with which the poterion was filled.

Gerard, referring to the herb in salads and wine, said: "It is thought to make the hart merry and glad, as also being put into wine, to which it yeeldeth a certaine grace in the drinking."

The Roman Pliny advised a decoction of Burnet beaten up with

Burnet

honey for several disorders, and among its old and much valued medicinal attributes was the belief in its protective power against the infection of the Plague and other contagious diseases. It was also judged to be a great healer of wounds, inward and outward, used as a drink or ointment; and it cured the Tudors' gout and rheumatism. Today it is used as an astringent medicine.

Salad Burnet is perennial and a member of the Rose family, Rosaceae. It grows wild and rather stunted on chalk downs in the English southern counties, where it provides valuable evergreen pastures for sheep. It prefers a rather dryish soil and when grown as a salad herb the flower-stems should be cut down and the leaves should be used when young and tender.

CARAWAY

Pale-faced girls were advised to take Caraway by the Greek physician Dioscorides. Apart from its many medicinal uses, Caraway was one of the most popular of herbs in classic times. Root, leaf and fruit ("seeds") were employed. The long thick roots like little parsnips were mixed with milk and made into bread, which was probably Julius Caesar's "chara," part of the rations of Roman soldiers; they were eaten as a vegetable, and the leaves went into salads and soups. Caraway seeds yielded the valuable medicinal oil and were liked as flavouring for a great many dishes, sweets, dessert and wines. The ancient Arabs also esteemed this plant, and their name for the seeds, *Karawya*, was probably the origin of the name Caraway.

Early in the 17th century, Parkinson said: "The seed is much used to be put among baked fruit, or into bread, cakes, etc., to give them a relish. It is also made into comfites and taken for cold or wind in the body, which also are served to the table with fruit." He declared the young roots to be superior in flavour to Parsnips.

Caraway-seed cake was for ages a traditional part of the farm-labourers' feasts given at the end of wheat-sowing. In Germany, cheeses, cabbage, soups and bread are flavoured with Caraway; it is also used to flavour a popular bread made in Norway and Sweden. The liqueur "Kummel" is made from Caraway, and it flavours "L'Huile de Vénus" and several other cordials.

According to an old superstition, Caraway was supposed to have the power of holding, it prevented thieves from taking anything which

Caraway

contained it, and it held lovers from straying in their affections after taking a love-potion which was mixed with it. (It certainly prevents fowls and pigeons from straying if they are provided with a piece of dough baked with Caraway seeds in it.)

Caraway's proper name, *Carum carvi*, comes from Caria, a district in Asia Minor where it was discovered. It is a biennial herb about two feet tall, a member of the aromatic Umbelliferae family, with umbels of white flowers in June, and ferny leaves resembling those of Cow Parsley. The seeds may be sown in spring or autumn, and it is not fussy about soil.

CLOVE CARNATION

The Clove Carnation is one of the oldest of garden flowers and was grown in the oldest herb gardens. As the offspring of a wild type found in the south of Europe, its possibilities were discovered and exploited at an early date. Pliny, writing about the plant, said it was found in Spain in the days of Augustus Caesar; he called it the "cantabrica" and said it was used by the Spaniards to spice their beverages. The Romans, too, cultivated it and wove the flowers into their festive crowns and garlands; they employed them to give their spicy flavour to wines and cups, and also made wine from them (today the Carnation is an ingredient of the liqueur Chartreuse).

It is possible that the Clove Carnation first came to Britain along with the numerous plants brought here by the Roman settlers, and it was certainly a well-loved familiar plant in the Middle Ages. In the reign of Edward III, Chaucer referred to its then common uses:

> "And many a clowe-gilofre;
> And notemuge to putte in ale,
> Whether it be moyste or stale,
> Or for to leye in cofre."

The "clowe-gilofre" or Clove Carnation, as well as spicing ale, was used fresh or dried to lay in coffers or clothes-presses with other aromatic herbs, to "sweeten" clothes.

Evidence of the affection in which this fragrant flower was held can be seen in many an ancient picture and illuminated manuscript. There it appears sometimes clasped in fingers to be often "smelled to," or it is lovingly painted in a margin, or the blooms are laid in some interior ready to be picked up and enjoyed by a nearby medieval figure. It was a more than ordinarily popular motif for old decorations such as embroideries and tapestries. Sprays of Carnations rioted over Tudor garments, cushions, table-carpets, prayer-books and hangings. The Stuarts' designs were equally full of these flowers as were those of later periods. Some of the adaptations were obviously copies from old Persian conceptions, for the Persians had long used the Carnation to decorate their special tiles and other objects.

The old names "Gillyvors," "Gilliflower" or "Gilloflower" were a corruption of the Carnation's specific Latin name, *Caryophyllum*, meaning a clove, an allusion to the flower's clove-like scent, and when these foreign spices were too expensive for ordinary uses the flowers were employed as their flavouring substitute. The popular name, Carnation, referring to their colour, was corrupted into "coronation," because of the ancient use of the blooms in the betrothal crowns or chaplets, worn by lovers as the emblems of the engagement of both their hearts and hands. The name Carnation was first used in 1578, in Henry Lyte's translation of the famous *Histoire des Plantes*, compiled by Rembert Dodoens, of Antwerp, in 1557. The generic name, *Dianthus*, came from the Greek, *dios*, a god, and *anthos*, a flower, "divine flower."

The Clove Carnation was grown to provide petals to be dried for potpourris, sachets and scented cushions. And being edible, they decorated salads and other dishes, were candied, and were the "soppes in wine" often referred to by old writers, when the flowers were dropped into mulled wine or ale.

These rich red Carnations were the ones cultivated in herb gardens, while the fancy kinds which were evolved at an early date were the pride of the pleasure grounds, and were known in a great variety of colours and patternings. Yellow varieties were described by Gerard as being introduced by·Master Lete about 1580. In *The Winter's Tale* Shakespeare makes Perdita speak of "streaked gilivors" as though these "painted ladies" (as they were called) were quite common in Tudor gardens.

In his *Paradisi in Sole Paradisus Terrestris* (1629) Parkinson listed nineteen kinds of Carnations and thirty sorts of Pinks. These flowers, it is said, were the favourite blooms of Charles I's Queen Henrietta Maria, and this royal preference made them extremely fashionable, and, as they were particularly adaptable, they were bred into almost countless

Clove Carnation

variations and "conceits," but the old Red Clove Carnation remained the standby in the housewife's kitchen garden.

This splendid Carnation is one of the easiest to grow in any good non-acid soil. It is very hardy and can be increased by layerings or cuttings. A few pea-sticks unobtrusively placed will hold up the flower stems, which are apt to fall as the heavy blooms open.

CHAMOMILE

Of Chamomile, Turner said: "It will restore a man to hys color shortly yf a man after the longe use of the bathe drynke of it after he is come forthe out of the bathe." And, as an historical fact: "Thys herbe was consecrated by the wyse men of Egypt unto the Sonne and was rekened to be the only remedy for all agues."

The name of the genus *Anthemis* is from the Greek word for a flower. The name Chamomile comes from the Greek, *khamai*, on the ground, and *melon*, apple, that is a ground apple, because of its scent. The Spaniards knew it as *manzanilla*, a little apple, and gave this name to a very light sherry which was flavoured with the herb. Chamomile is also used in the making of some Vermouths.

The name Chamomile is loosely given to several plants; but the true type that is grown for use, dried or fresh, to make Chamomile tea, shampoos for blondes, fomentations or scented lawns, is *Anthemis nobilis*. The specific name, noble, was bestowed on the herb because it bore large flowers for so tiny a plant. This kind has become familiarly known as the Roman Chamomile, for no better reason than because in the 16th century a German writer, visiting Italy, found it growing near Rome. This is the *Anthemis* described by Dioscorides and every other herb-minded physician from earliest times. It is one of the oldest of physic herbs, and was grown in most gardens for use as a common domestic medicine. The soothing, sedative tea was brewed almost daily to drink for pleasure and for most human upsets. It was particularly effective for curing nightmares, it cooled the feverish patient, and, when necessary, helped the victims of delirium tremens. Lotions were made of Chamomile for calming aching teeth and ears and comforting neuralgic pains, and it was used in home-brewed herb beers.

Culpepper's long list of ailments relieved by Chamomile included agues "from flegm or melancholy, or from inflammation of the bowels,"

Chamomile

and he said: "There is nothing more profitable to the sides and region of the liver and spleen than it." He recommended it for weariness, all pains, strained sinews, swellings, also for jaundice and dropsy and many other complaints. In his *Earthly Paradise* (1656), Parkinson wrote: "Camomil is put to divers and sundry uses, both for pleasure and profit, both for the sick and the sound, in bathing to comfort and strengthen the sound and to ease pains in the diseased."

This benevolent Chamomile grows wild over much of Europe and the temperate regions of Asia. It is found wild in some English southern counties in places where the soil is light and sandy. Perhaps, long ago it was more plentiful, as in the 16th century William Turner described it, saying: "This herbe is scarce in Germany but in England it is so plenteous that it groweth not only in gardynes but also VIII mile above London, it groweth in the wylde felde, in Rychmonde grene, in Brantfurd grene."

Chamomile's aromatic odour, which was pleasant when trodden on the carpetless floors as a medieval strewing herb, was also enjoyed in Tudor and Stuart gardens and those of later periods. Walks and small lawns were planted with the herb that liked to be pressed into the ground:

> "Like a Camomile bed—
> The more it is trodden
> The more it will spread."

Anthemis nobilis is low-growing and creeping, with jointed, fibrous perennial roots. The tufted, downy, greyish-green, feathery foliage forms mats of plush-like texture. It is of the Daisy-flowered family, Compositae, and there are both single- and double-flowered forms. The double kind is recommended for medicinal purposes, as the strong alkali in the single flowers is injurious to the stomach coating. Today, the plants are variable and the double form is apt to revert to single flowers.

When making a Chamomile path or lawn, the site must be thoroughly dug and cleared of perennial weed roots. The soil should be mixed with compost and, where necessary, coarse sand. The bed must be trodden firm and raked level. The plantlets need to be set six inches apart, with their roots well down and the crowns on the surface. The first cuttings must be done with sharp shears, and flowering must be checked. When the beds are established, a mower may be used with the blades set high.

CHERVIL

Chervil is one of the most deliciously flavoured of culinary herbs; it is the *Cerfeuil* of the French, and very important in their herb bouquet, "Fines Herbes." All continental cooks require it almost daily and grow it in their kitchen gardens, but it is seldom seen in English ones. This is our loss, as apart from the shrubby evergreen herbs such as Sage, Rosemary, Thyme, etc., Chervil is one of the few flavouring plants which survive our winters in the open ground to be available fresh for use throughout the year. Its savoury taste is often rather imaginatively described as resembling that of Caraway, but it has a rich individual one of its own which blends well with meat or fish. A famous continental soup is made with Chervil and others are flavoured with it; the leaves are chopped into salads and flavour dressings; it goes into savoury puddings and butters; it makes a tasty herb vinegar; it flavours stews and any savoury dish, and it is sprinkled as a garnish for the same purposes as Parsley is generally used in Britain.

Chervil is an annual herb growing up to eighteen inches high, with finely-cut, fern-like leaves of a fresh bright green colour that turns as they fade to a delightful purplish-pink. The tiny white flowers, typical of its family, Umbelliferae, are borne in umbels. Its generic name, *Anthriscus*, was given by Pliny, and the specific name, *cerefolium*, means waxy, and refers to the texture of the leaves. The plant has long been enjoyed as a wholesome culinary herb but has no great medicinal reputation beyond the ancient use of the roots as a soothing, warming dish for chilled stomachs. Chervil is a native of southern Europe and the Levant.

Chervil is rather like a small Sweet Cicely and has become so closely associated with it that in English herb-lore Sweet Cicely is sometimes called Great Chervil, Sweet Chervil, and Cow Chervil.

Although Chervil is an annual herb and easy to cultivate, the seeds quickly lose their germinating power, and bought seed is often disappointing. It is a good plan, therefore, to start with small plantlets from a nursery, then they can sow their own seeds immediately they ripen, and will eventually form a useful colony. It likes a fairly rich moisture-holding soil and a little shade.

Chervil

CHIVES

The Chive, resembling a tiny Onion, is rarely alone for long enough to be regarded as an individual, as it rapidly makes a dense cluster of kindred bulbs and is generally referred to in the plural. Chives, "of quick rellish," were always a favourite culinary herb. Parkinson described them growing in his garden, and they were cultivated in most private gardens for convenient use, and in all market gardens to be sold in great quantities in ancient towns.

From earliest times, the Chive's popularity was widespread as it grew wild over most of the northern hemisphere from Siberia, Corsica, Greece, Italy, southern Sweden and North America. It was introduced into China about 2,000 years ago, where it was valued as an antidote to poisons and a remedy for bleeding. It is only found wild in the northern and western counties of England and Wales and in Oxfordshire.

Only the hollow grass-like leaves are used of this little relation of the robust, triumphant Onion (which was given divine honours in ancient Egypt). Their mild, delicate oniony flavour goes well with any savoury dish and gives zest to a salad. Chives have an antiseptic quality, for they contain the volatile oil rich in sulphur that is characteristic of all the Onion tribe, the *Alliums*, whose name originated as the Latin name for Garlic, and is now given to the entire Onion family. Chive's specific name, *schoenoprasum*, was the old Greek name for the Leek. This odorous group belongs to the Lily order, Liliaceae.

Chives may be grown as a neat edging to a herb bed where they look like opulent Thrifts. Their flowers are massed into a globular bunch of mauve-pink blossoms topping a slender stem about ten inches high. These should be discouraged or the leaves will toughen. The leaves for use should be cut close to the ground and are soon replaced. The clumps should be divided each year and reset in bunches of about nine bulbs. Chives like a rich light soil.

COMFREY

Two excellent reasons for growing Comfrey are its appearance and the fritters that can be made from its leaves. The common wild Comfrey with dusky purple or creamy-yellow blooms is a dim plant compared with the Caucasian type, with brilliant gentian-blue flowers borne on three-foot-high stems. It has all the lovely characteristics of Comfreys,

Chives

Comfrey

and the racemes of tubular blossoms are produced in pairs, hanging along one side of the curved "scorpion" stem, gradually tapering from fully expanded bells to the tiny bud at the extremity. The plant is lush, rough and hairy. This Caucasian Comfrey's name is *Symphytum Caucasicum*, and there is a Russian type, *S. peregrinum*, four feet tall with pale pure-blue flowers; these two Comfreys make a beautiful group and they bloom from spring to autumn.

From ancient times Comfrey was valued for its curative qualities by Dioscorides, by Pliny, and by many succeeding physicians. It was held to be an effective vulnerary herb, a healer of chronic wounds, burns and broken bones. Its constituent, Allantoin, a remedy for external and internal ulcers, is now also artificially made for various modern medical treatments.

The popular name Comfrey is perhaps a corruption of the Latin *confervere*, to grow together (of fractures), and the botanical name *Symphytum* comes from the Greek *sumphuo*, unite. It is of the Boraginaceae family and because of this tribe's ability to produce together both pink and blue flowers, Comfrey is sometimes called "Abraham, Isaac and Jacob." Its many other local names, such as Knit Bone, Bruisewort, in general refer to its old rustic reputation. It was grown in herb gardens for home-doctoring; the leaves and roots, which contained much mucilage, were particularly useful for making soothing fomentations to reduce swellings, and a decoction was brewed for drinking to relieve cases of dysentery, diarrhoea and consumption. The tender young leaves were also fancied as a tasty vegetable and to flavour cakes and puddings. A delicious Comfrey fritter is made in Bavaria and has a place in German cookery books.

Comfreys will grow in any good soil that is moistish in summer; they prefer a little shade from trees, rather than full sun. They are perennial plants and readily grow from pieces of root cut from established plants.

CORIANDER

According to a Chinese belief, Coriander seeds had the power of bestowing immortality. The attractive bright-green shining plant is a very old culinary herb and has eventually travelled as far as Peru to make its greatest conquest. The Peruvians became so fond of it that they flavoured nearly all their dishes with the leaves or seeds. Egyptian cooks, too, use the leaves in soups. Long ago, Pliny maintained that the best

Coriander

Coriander seeds were imported from Egypt to ancient Rome. The plant is indigenous to southern Europe, but has long been used in the East where the seeds became an ingredient of Indian curry powder, and the leaves were important to several Indian dishes. The Romans brought Coriander to Britain as a favourite aromatic spice, and it was happy enough to establish itself as a semi-wild plant in some eastern counties. At one time it was commercially grown in Essex for the distillers of gin, and as a drug for veterinary surgeons to use for their cattle patients.

Describing Coriander, Gerard said: "The common kind of Coriander is a very striking herb, it has a round stalk full of branches, two feet long. The leaves are almost like the leaves of the Parsley, but later on become more jagged, almost like the leaves of Fumitorie, but a deal smaller and tenderer. The flowers are white and grow in round tassels like Dill." The green seed-heads are very decorative.

Coriander is an annual to grow from seed sown either in September or April. The leaves are often liked in salads, stews and soups, and the seeds are good in bread or cakes and for flavouring jelly and other sweets. Round comfits of pink and white are made from the seeds by some confectioners.

Coriandrum sativum, which is the herb's proper name, alludes to its horrid smell, the generic name being derived from the Greek *koris*, a bug. When the seeds fully ripen, the smell and taste become pleasantly aromatic, and the longer they are kept the more the flavour improves.

DANDELION

The Dandelion may appear an odd subject in a book suggesting plants to furnish a herb garden and contribute to the cook's resources. This plant, which is usually regarded as an obstinate persistent "weed," with flat golden-rayed blooms and round, downy seedheads, is really a valuable salad herb and vegetable, with other uses.

The Dandelion was once as highly esteemed in Britain as it is today on the Continent, particularly in France, where it is grown commercially to be sold in the markets. Its food value is impressive; it has a high content of Vitamin A; at least four times more Vitamin C than lettuce; it has more iron than spinach, and is rich in potassium. The Dandelion's medicinal uses are chiefly for stimulating the bladder and kidneys, as a general tonic, a stimulant and gentle aperient, and it is prescribed for disorders of the liver; so that its use as a food can only be beneficial.

Dandelion

The young tender leaves are a pleasant and health-giving addition to salads, as they taste rather like endive and are commonly used in French spring salads. As a vegetable they are good when boiled like spinach, with very little water, then drained, seasoned with salt and pepper, and shaken in butter before serving very hot. A squeeze of lemon juice, a sprinkling of Chives or chopped Garlic may be added to the leaves when cooked. The young leaves, torn to pieces, not cut, make appetizing sandwiches, with either a little lemon juice on them or a few drops of Worcester Sauce on the bread and butter. The leaves may be blanched by placing plant-pots over them and covering the drainage holes with stones to exclude all light, but when paled, many of the virtues are destroyed and they are not so beneficial as the green leaves.

Dandelion coffee is made from the roasted roots and is entirely wholesome and more digestible than real coffee. It may be drunk as a general stimulant. To make it, the roots of two-year-old plants are dug in autumn when they are plump with food reserves, then, when the crowns are cut away, they are washed and dried in a cool oven. They can be stored for a few months in a dry place, in tins, to prevent attacks from mould or maggots. When required they are roasted to a light coffee brown and ground as coffee.

The Dandelion is at home everywhere in the north temperate zone, and the commonest of its popular names refer to the lion's tooth, as in its old Latin name *Dens leonis*, in the French *Dent de lion*, and the English corruption Dandelion. It is not clear whether the root, the flower or the toothed-leaves are supposed to resemble lion's teeth. The *Ortus Sanitatis* (1485) offers a doubtful answer: "The Herb was much employed by Master Wilhemus, a surgeon, who on account of its virtues, likened it to a lion's tooth . . ." Some of its local names are easier to explain such as the clock ones, "Fairy Clock," "Shepherd's Clock," etc., each puff counting as an hour while blowing away the fluffy seeds. "Swine Snout" and the "Priest's Crown" of the Middle Ages both refer to the bare disc after the seeds have gone, resembling a pig's snout or the once familiar sight of a monk's shaven head. "Wet-a-Bed" and its variations in several languages and dialects alluded to the effect of an overdose of the medicine.

The plant's proper name, *Taraxacum*, from a Greek word, stir up or alter, refers to the curative effects. The specific name *officinale*, of the herbal shops, was given to all official herbs. Dandelion belongs to the Daisy family, Compositae.

According to John Evelyn, Hecate entertained Theseus with this ancient salad herb. Evelyn was a great salad-fancier in the days when they were vastly important. James II's head cook stipulated at least thirty-two ingredients in an ordinary salad and many more in a "brave sallet" and Dandelion leaves were usually included. Country people made Dandelion beer from the leaves, and a light sherry-like wine from the flowers, both drinks being excellent tonics and good for the blood.

A row or two of Dandelions is as practical a salad crop as any and the plants last two or three years, making lush growth when grown in a bed of good deep soil. The broad-leaved variety should be chosen. The flowers must be removed, as if allowed to seed they become a nuisance.

DILL

Dill was a magician's herb, used in their spells, and in their charms to thwart witches:

> "There with her Vervain and her Dill,
> That hindereth Witches of their Will."

wrote Drayton in the 17th century.

It was the comforting herb, the ancient soothing one, from its old Norse name *Dilla*, meaning to lull, to the Dill-water that has quieted uncomfortable babies probably since prehistoric times. Dill's medicinal virtue has long been valued as an entirely safe remedy for relieving flatulence at any age, and for settling disturbed stomachs and acting as a mild stimulant.

Dill was the Anethon of the Greek physician Dioscorides and prescribed by him for curing hiccough and flatulence. The Greeks used it in a variety of ways and burnt it as a perfume and incense. The Romans, too, according to Pliny, knew it well and enjoyed it. It would certainly be familiar as the plant grew wild in districts along the Mediterranean and in Southern Russia (and is particularly happy as a cornfield weed in Italy, Spain and Portugal).

Probably the earliest record of Dill used medicinally is in the ancient Egyptian medical papyrus of nearly 5,000 years ago, and by comparison its mention by Alfric, Archbishop of Canterbury, in his 10th-century vocabulary, seems fairly recent. Lyte, in his translation of Dodoens' herbal (1578), said that Dill was grown in all gardens amongst the worts and pot-herbs. And its superstitious uses were perhaps as much valued as its medicinal ones, for it was always a plant of good omen to be worn "for luck," especially by brides, who in some countries used to put a sprig in their shoes with a little salt and wear sprays of Dill at their weddings.

Culpepper said this herb was under the dominion of Mercury, and therefore it strengthened the brain, and that: "The Dill being boiled and drunk is good to ease swellings and pains, it also stayeth the belly and stomach from casting . . . It stayeth the hiccough . . . The seed is more use than the leaves, and more effectual to digest raw and viscous humours, and it is used in medicines that serve to expel wind and pains proceeding therefrom." His other uses for Dill were for plasters of its seed mixed with oil to dry up moist ulcers, and he advised oil of Dill as a sedative "To procure rest" as others had done long before, and as a few years later Swan wrote in his *Speculum Mundi*: "It procureth sleep sound and secure." Dill was a boon to the sleepless.

Dill is a hardy annual growing about two feet tall. The plant is very like Fennel with the same fine feathery leaves, but it has usually only one stem whereas Fennel is branching. Dill's flavour is rather like that of Anise but cooler and more subtle. It belongs to the Umbelliferae family, bearing umbels of small yellow flowers. The "seeds" are so light that 25,000 are needed to weigh one ounce, so that in a small garden the plant is most valuable for its leaves, which are good in salads and many other dishes.

On the Continent Dill is a favourite culinary herb; both the leaves and the seeds are used in various ways, they give their spicy flavour to soups, sauces and stews, and as a garnish and sauce for fish, and in France the seeds are employed in cakes and confectionery. The Scandinavians also use Dill in several ways and are particularly fond of it boiled with new potatoes and peas to flavour and garnish them, as we use Mint. An excellent aromatic vinegar can be made by soaking Dill seeds in white wine vinegar for a week before use. This adds relish to salad dressings and can be blended into other sauces.

Dill has been most appreciated for its flavour in pickling such things as Cucumbers, Gherkins and Cauliflowers. Some of the early cooks have left their recipes for the processes they used, and some old writers have recorded their liking for the results. Joseph Cooper, King Charles I's cook (1640), gave his recipe in his *Receipt Book*, "To Pickle Cucumbers in Dill." And in John Evelyn's *Acetaria* (1680), a book about

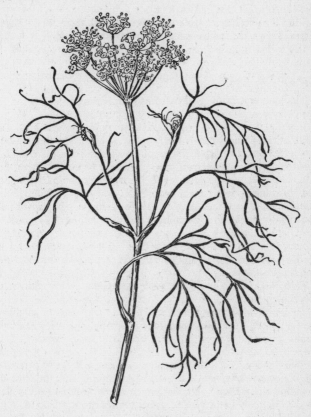

Dill

"Sallets," on which he was an authority, there is his method for making "Dill and Collyflower Pickle."

Dill's botanical name *Peucedanum* was given to the plant by Hippocrates; its specific name, *graveolens*, means strong-smelling.

Dill is easy to grow from seed sown in spring in any good soil.

ELDER

There are not many gardens without an Elder tree, though it may not have been planted, as in the past, to frustrate witches.

It was regarded as a powerful rather awesome tree, and it was once believed that Christ's cross was made from its wood. But this old belief was unacceptable to Gerard, who said the Judas Tree (*Cercis siliquastrum*) was the "tree whereon Judas did hange himselfe." From these ideas and countless other superstitions that were attached to it, the Elder was highly respected and cherished. And as an infallible protection against all evil, including lightning's terrors, it was planted in all gardens, by stables to protect cattle and in churchyards to guard the dead. It was a valuable asset to any household as no other tree or plant provided so many good things as the Elder. Its wood, leaves, flowers and berries all had their uses, and all parts had medicinal virtues and were safe and beneficial.

Elder was extolled by all ancient physicians, and Evelyn said: "If the medicinal properties of its leaves, bark and berries were fully known, I cannot tell what our countryman could ail for which he might not fetch a remedy from every hedge, either for sickness, or wounds." And it was said that the great physician Boerhaave never passed an Elder without raising his hat.

Both the Greeks and the Romans knew Elder well. It was prescribed by Hippocrates for several illnesses, and the Romans made their hair-dye from its berries. Pliny and other ancient writers referred to it as *Sambucus*, the tree's Latin generic name, derived from the Latin word, *sambuca*, a Roman musical instrument that was probably made from Elder wood. Pliny wrote of its medical uses and also said the best flutes and pipes were those made from Elder trees which had grown where no cock-crows could be heard. He mentioned boys' whistles made from the hollow branches. And, to pass from ancient Rome to Britain many centuries later, Culpepper said: "It is needless to write any description of this, since every boy that plays with a pop-gun will not mistake

Elder

another tree for the Elder." He also mentioned the black hair-dye made from the berries boiled in wine.

The Elder is an attractive small tree, and with its flat masses of cream, scented blossoms that change to heavy bunches of juicy black-purple berries, it is typical of English summers.

Its annual uses can begin with taking some young shoots in May, to make an old delicious "Pickle in imitation of Indian Bamboo." The leaves of the *Sambucus* are used in the manufacture of a familiar domestic, green-coloured, healing ointment. They are repellent to flies and other insects, and an infusion made from them and dabbed on the skin prevents attacks by mosquitoes and midges. They were also considered effective for keeping mice from larders.

The flowers smell and taste of muscatel grapes, and many delicious things can be made from them such as fritters, Elder Milk, light batters, and one of the most delectable of all home-made wines, apart from the easily made and surprisingly pleasant fizzy, summer drink "Elder-flower Champagne." Elder-flower Water has always been known for its refining and soothing effect on the complexion.

The berries have a number of uses; they make a rich addition to apple pies; they are good when spiced for tarts and pies; they mix well with stewed fruit such as rhubarb, apples and cooking pears; alone or with crab-apples they produce a fine jelly, and with vegetable marrow, with apples or alone they make a good jam.

Elder-berry wine, if well made, resembles port or claret according to the method of making. Elder-berry syrup is excellent with hot water to relieve a cold. These berries are used in great quantities as the basis of inferior red wines, particularly claret, port and Bordeaux.

As the berries possess valuable medicinal qualities, wine and other things made from them are entirely beneficial, and were at one time valued for relieving rheumatic and nerve pains, dropsy and gout among other ailments, but most likely they were usually taken for pleasure.

More than one Elder tree is needed in a garden if all the Elder's culinary possibilities are to be enjoyed, as when full use is made of the blossoms all the opportunities offered by the juicy berries are lost.

Elders appear to grow and flourish anywhere in reasonably good soil in a fairly sunny position.

FENNEL

The decorative Fennel growing like a fountain of feathery leaves up to six feet high was called *Marathron* by the Greeks, from *maraino*, grow thin. Apart from its slimming powers, they believed it gave strength, courage and long life. The Romans gave Fennel its generic name, *Foeniculum*, from *foenum*, hay. This was corrupted in the Middle Ages into *Fanculum*, then Fenkel, which was often used.

Fennel was an ancient culinary and medicinal herb, and the Romans made much use of it, eating root, stem, leaf and seeds; they served it raw as a salad herb and cooked as a vegetable, and seeds flavoured bread, cakes, soups and other dishes. Its use in Roman medicines was recorded by Pliny who listed twenty-two ailments for which Fennel was considered an effective treatment.

Charlemagne ordered Fennel's cultivation on all imperial farms, and its health-giving products were listed in a 10th-century Spanish agricultural record. Fennel's benefit to the eyes was a persistent belief; Pliny recorded that serpents sharpened their sight with the juice by rubbing against the plant. Most of the old herbalists held the same belief in its help to clear vision.

When all herbs were regarded as endowed with certain powers, Fennel's were thought to be benevolent and opposed to any witchcraft. Bed-chambers were protected by stuffing the key-holes with it to prevent malignant spirits entering and disturbing the sleepers. Fennel was included in the protective garlands which were hung over doors on Midsummer Eve, the witches' most potent season.

Fennel's culinary and medicinal uses were well known in Anglo-Saxon England and they are found in many herbals of that period. In the 11th century, Edward I's household accounts gave eight and a half pounds of Fennel for a month's supply. It was generally used to cook with fish that had been salted for winter storage. It appeared in 14th-century writings, and Gerard described it in 1597. Parkinson, in 1640, said its culinary use originated in Italy. "The leaves, seede and rootes are both for meate and medicine; the Italians especially doe much delight in the use thereof, and therefore transplant and whiten it, to make it more tender to please the taste, which being sweete and somewhat hot helpeth to digest the crude qualitie of fish and other viscous meats. We use it to lay upon fish or to boyle it therewith and with divers other things, as also the seeds in bread and other things." William

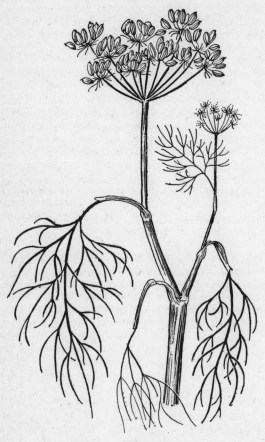

Fennel

Coles, writing ten years later, gave another English use of Fennel as the ancient slimming herb, "both the seeds, leaves and root of our Garden Fennel are much used in drinks and broths for those that are grown fat, to abate their unwieldiness and cause them to grow more gaunt and lank." It has been suggested that, as Shakespeare was often topical, Ophelia perhaps offered her Fennel to a fat actor.

Culpepper had previously given his opinion of Fennel's medicinal uses which covered an astonishing variety of ills and included the neutralzing of mushroom poison. He liked the herb with fish and said: "One good old custom is not yet left off, viz., to boil fennel with fish, for it consumes the phlegmatic humour which fish most plentifully afford and annoy the body with, though few that use it know wherefore they do it." Maybe they just liked the flavour as the herb continues to be one of the most popular to accompany fish, particularly on the Continent. There the seeds still flavour cakes and bread, and Roman bakers place sprays of the leaves under loaves while baking to give them a pleasant taste. In Italy, the peeled stems, *cartucci*, are still served as salad with vinegar and pepper dressing. A very old English recipe gave instructions for boiling young Fennel stems like "Sparragrass" and serving them with butter and vinegar.

Among Fennel's many useful aids to man was its ability to repel his insect pests; being disliked by the fleas that were always troublesome, it was strewn in chambers and placed in beds. And it provided one of the comforting ingredients of infants' "gripe-water."

Fennel's flavour, like that of most herbs, is difficult to describe; it rather resembles a mixture of Aniseed, Chervil and Parsley. It is a Mediterranean plant that has become naturalized in many parts of Europe and Britain. It grows in any good soil in the sun. It is a fine aromatic perennial of the Umbelliferae family, with umbels of yellow flowers.

GARLIC

Considering Garlic's past it is evident that throughout man's history its smell prevailed over all others. Man spread this precious herb around his world such a long time ago that no one can say for certain where Garlic originated. Some think south-west Siberia, and it may have accompanied the earliest nomads. By the time history was recorded, Garlic was happily established throughout southern Europe and was cultivated in every community. It was liked as a food, valued as a medicine and reverenced as a mystical herb. In Egypt, according to Pliny, the Garlic and Onion were addressed as deities when oaths were taken. In parts of Lower Egypt they were too divine to be eaten and were worshipped.

Garlic was the main part of the Israelites' diet in Egypt, as it was of the labourers employed by Cheops in the building of his pyramid. Great quantities were issued to the Greek and Roman soldiers and sailors. And all rural classes in Europe and north Africa ate it as one of their chief foods.

The Greeks considered Garlic fitting food for a goddess and placed it on piles of stones at cross-roads, as a supper for Hecate (the triple deity, Phoebe in heaven, Diana on earth and Proserpine, or Hecate, in hell).

Garlic's use as a culinary herb always had its advocates and critics. The Greek poet Homer made it part of the feast served by Nestor, the wisest hero of the Trojan war, to his guest Machaon; and he attributed to Garlic Ulysses' lucky escape from being changed into a pig by Circe, as were all his companions. But in ancient Greece no one having eaten Garlic was allowed to enter the temples of Cybele. The Roman Horace detested Garlic and said it was "more poisonous than Hemlock" and that it had made him ill at the table of Maecenas. He considered that the smell of Garlic was vulgar—anticipating Shakespeare's references to the mob in *Coriolanus* and *Measure for Measure*, as well as in *A Midsummer Night's Dream*: "And, most dear actors, eat no onions nor garlic, for we are to utter sweet breath."

Country people everywhere were not only addicted to Garlic as a food, but believed its application to be cooling, especially in districts where the hot desert winds made field-work uncomfortable. This custom was alluded to in a travel book of a century ago: "The people in places where the Simoon is frequent, eat Garlic and rub their lips and noses with it when they go out in the heat of the summer to prevent their suffering from the Simoon." Alexander Neckham, a 12th-century English writer, recommended Garlic for much the same purpose.

Garlic's medicinal virtues were recognized at an early date. Pliny gave an exceedingly long list of its curative uses, and Galen praised it as the rustic's "Theriac" or "heal all." Chaucer and the old writers referred to it in that sense—"Poor Man's Treacle" (Latin, *theriacus*, antidote). Dioscorides prescribed it especially for clearing the voice.

Physicians and writers many centuries later had much to say of

Garlic

Garlic. In his *Book of Simples*, 1562, the understanding William Bullein said it was a gross kind of medicine and very unpleasant for "fayre Ladyes" who, he said, "preferre sweete breathes before gentle wordes." The astrological-minded Culpepper wrote: "Mars owns this herb" and gave an impressive list of complaints it would relieve, and he added: "But the Garlic hath some peculiar vertues besides the former, viz. it hath a special quality to discuss the inconveniences coming by corrupt and stinking waters." Garlic is disinfectant and antiseptic (tons of Garlic were used to treat wounds during the 1914–18 war). It is interesting that Garlic was the main ingredient in the famous "Four Thieves' Vinegar," a remedy used during an outbreak of plague in Marseilles in 1722. Four convicted thieves maintained that it had protected them from infection whilst robbing the dead bodies of the epidemic's victims. During an outbreak of an infectious fever in certain London slums early in the 19th century, the French priests who ate Garlic at every meal were able to minister to the victims with safety, whereas the English clergy caught the infection.

Garlic, the "Spear Leek" with a long spear-like spath, is *Allium sativum*, of the Liliaceae order. Like most of the Onion tribe, it likes a well-drained bed of rich open soil in a sunny position. The "cloves" should be planted in March, one inch deep and six inches apart.

HYSSOP

A man who was violently kicked on the thigh by a horse was poulticed with boiled Hyssop and the pain instantly ceased, and within a few hours no bruises could be seen. John Ray, who compiled the first British Flora (1670), related this spectacular cure by Hyssop, which was always famed for removing such discolorations. The green leaves too, when bruised and applied to cuts, healed them quickly.

Hyssop has other useful virtues, but it would be worth growing in any garden if only for its attractive appearance and its scent, which is difficult to describe: it is warmly aromatic with a vague suggestion of oil of Lavender on Russian leather. Hyssop is a shrubby semi-evergreen herb, usually about two feet high. However, in the warm western counties of Devon and Cornwall where it is often used for making fragrant hedges in gardens, it reaches three to four feet in height. Hyssop hedges clip well into neat shapes, but of course most of the flower sprays are lost. When left unclipped, it tends in time to sprawl

Hyssop

low down over a large area, even up to four feet across. The narrow lance-shaped leaves are a darkish green and it bears its deep Gentian blue two-lipped flowers in whorls along the ends of the sprays. There are also varieties of this Hyssop bearing pink, purple and white flowers.

Like Rosemary, Lavender, Thyme, etc., Hyssop is of the Labiatae family, and has the same square woody stems. Its botanical name is *Hyssopus officinalis*. The specific name means of the herbal shops, but the generic name came from the Greek hussopos used by Dioscorides in his *Materia Medica*, and is thought probably to be of Hebrew origin. It was *azob*, a holy herb, used by the Hebrews and others, to cleanse sacred places. It was referred to over 2,000 years ago in the fifty-first Psalm, the Hebrew hymn, "Purge me with hyssop and I shall be clean." Although some authorities now say the translation is doubtful and the plant was either Marjoram or Caper-Plant, Hyssop would surely be a worthier herb for scenting temples, and later, churches, and it was certainly used in the Middle Ages for strewing in palaces, banqueting halls and grand houses.

The leaves, flowers and stems of *Hyssopus officinalis* yield by distillation a fine odorous oil which is used by perfumers and is of even greater value than oil from Lavender. The plant's special healing virtues are in its particular volatile oil which is also gently stimulating and good for relieving flatulence. The old-fashioned tea made from the fresh green tips was a pleasurable remedy for rheumatism, anaemia and other complaints, in particular those of the chest and lungs. Gerard had faith in "a decoction of Hyssope made with figges, water, honey and rue, and drunken, helpeth the old cough."

As a culinary herb, Hyssop is a good rich flavouring for soups, stews and other meat dishes, and it was once much liked in stuffings, pies and sausages, but its taste is so potent that only a few leaves are required. A sprinkling of the crushed dried leaves or of minced fresh ones is excellent on salads. And as the herb keeps its scent when dried, it is a great asset in pot-pourris and delightful in washing-bags. Hyssop baths used to be recommended for the relief of rheumatic pains.

Hyssop is found growing wild in rocky places and, romantically, among ruins in Palestine and southern Europe. It revels in warm sunshine and is exceedingly attractive to bees, whose resulting honey is especially good. It is possible that the Romans brought the herb to Britain, and it was certainly grown here in all herb gardens from early times. It can be seen happily naturalized on the ruins of the ancient Cistercian Abbey of Beaulieu, in Hampshire.

Hyssop likes a well-drained bed of good light soil in a warm and sunny situation. New plants can be raised from green cuttings taken in summer, or from seeds sown outside in early May. This herb needs little attention beyond an occasional cutting back to prevent its becoming too lax. When grown as an aromatic hedge, the necessary clipping into shape should be done in March.

There is a charming dwarf Hyssop, *H. aristatus*, with brilliant blue flowers and of compact growth, reaching about fifteen inches high. This is an ideal plant for walls or pockets in the rock garden and for setting in sunny corners between paving stones.

LAVENDER

One derivation of the name *Lavandula* is from the Latin *lavo* or *lavare*, to wash. The elegant Greeks and Romans used this aromatic herb as a bath perfume and to relieve fatigue and stiff joints. The Romans never used it in their chaplets and garlands as they considered it too dangerous, being, they believed, a favourite haunt of the deadly asp.

Several types of Lavender native to the Mediterranean regions were employed in ancient times, but the old writers seldom distinguished between them. There was the little shrub with dark purple flowers, *L. stoechas* (French Lavender), that grew in abundance on the islands of Hyères near Toulon, which the ancient Romans called the "Stoechades" after the plant. This one was recorded by Dioscorides as growing off the coast of Gaul. It was a popular type for toilet purposes in the prosperous Mediterranean cities. The Spike Lavender, *L. spica*, with pointed flower spikes, grew in the mountainous districts of France and Spain. This was often confused with the Biblical Spikenard, one of the most costly unguents of the East, and the Romans, a small amount being priced at 300 Roman denarii (about £10). The best quality was made from an Indian plant with other ingredients and, according to Pliny, the "sincere" Nard was known by its red colour, its scent and delicious taste; it was kept in jars of alabaster or lead. There were many cheaper imitations, and doubtless Lavender provided some and became known as "Nard." Lavender was also expensive; in Pliny's day the blossoms cost 100 Roman denarii (£3 2s. 6d.) a pound.

The true Lavender, *L. vera*, which grew in the mountainous regions

D

of the countries bordering the western half of the Mediterranean, and had the most beautiful scent, was never distinguished by writers before the 12th century, when it appeared in the herbal of the abbess Hildegard, who lived near Bingen on the Rhine. It was Llafant to 13th-century Welsh physicians.

The Romans must have brought these favourite herbs to be enjoyed in Britain, but there is no record of their surviving here; maybe they brought the wrong kind, as only *L. vera* was really happy in Britain and was introduced into English gardens in 1568.

Before that date dried Lavender flowers were an import; pillows and sachets stuffed with them, and sweet washing water made from them were old pleasures. A cosy suggestion for their use was made by William Turner who wrote in his *New Herball* (1551): "I judge that the flowers of Lavender quilted in a cap and worne are good for all diseases of the head that come from a cold cause and that they comfort the braine very well."

Lavender's medicinal qualities had been appreciated for many centuries when Gerard and many other physicians and apothecaries wrote of them. Lavender was the panacea for many ills; it was a nerve stimulant, a reliever of aches and pains, sprains and rheumatism, a comforter of flatulence, and as an appetite provoking herb it went into food as a flavouring for many dishes. Powdered Lavender was served as a condiment, and Queen Elizabeth I much enjoyed conserve of Lavender which, it was said, was always on her table. The Pilgrim Fathers took the shrubs to America, but reported back home that "Lavender is not for this climate."

As *L. vera* was more than ordinarily successful in England it became known as "English Lavender." It so liked the climate that it produced a special quality here, making the oil from it about ten times more valuable than from plants grown elsewhere, and vast cultivation grounds were planted at Mitcham and other places in the southerly counties.

Parkinson, in his *Garden of Pleasure*, said Spike Lavender "is often called the Lesser Lavender or minor, and is called by some, Nardus Italica." He also mentioned "both the purple and the rare white (there is a kinde hereof that beareth white flowers and somewhat broader leaves, but it is very rare and seene but in a few places with us, because it is more tender and will not so well endure our cold Winters)." This was a favourite plant of Queen Henrietta Maria and it is said she grew great borders of it at her Wimbledon Manor.

Lavender

Lavender should be planted in a sunny position in a good soil that is well drained. Where the ground lacks sufficient alkaline content, limestone chippings should be incorporated. New plants are best propagated from small new shoots.

LOVAGE

It is difficult to understand why the ornamental Lovage is now seldom seen in English gardens. It is a handsome foliage plant and a generous source of leaves with a flavour resembling a mixture of Celery predominating over Parsley and Angelica. It used to be as popular a herb as any and was thought fine enough to be given a place in the flower borders where its dark green, polished leaves were both effective and pleasantly aromatic.

As a culinary herb, Lovage is excellent for giving its particularly enticing flavour to enrich soups, stews and other dishes, and its young tender leaves are good chopped up in salads. The herb is especially valuable in a garden when Celery is out of season, and the leaves dry well to store for winter use. The roots taste rather like Celeriac, and in some countries they are cooked, then sliced and eaten with an oil and vinegar dressing. The hollow stems are sometimes candied like Angelica's and used for the same purposes in confectionery, but they are not quite as good. The stems used to be blanched and boiled as a vegetable. A pleasantly aromatic tea was brewed from the dried or fresh leaves and regarded as being particularly good for young women.

Since the 14th century Lovage has been grown in English gardens and used for culinary as well as for medicinal purposes; and it was employed as a bath scent when such appetizing herbal perfumes were the fancy. It was a favourite flavouring and salad herb of the Tudors and Stuarts; and for many years an extremely popular cordial made from this herb with several others, was served at most inns, it was called "Lovage" and was believed to have a beneficial effect.

Lovage is a native of the Mediterranean countries, especially of the mountainous regions of southern France, northern Greece and the Balkans, and though it is sometimes found growing wild in Britain it is not considered to be indigenous here, but a garden escape of long ago, as it is probable that the Roman settlers originally introduced the plant for their use. Among the ancient Greeks and the Romans Lovage had a reputation as a pleasant and useful medicinal herb, and its antiseptic

Lovage

qualities would make it an effectively soothing treatment for certain ailments such as intestinal troubles and other disorders for which it was prescribed at an early date.

It is known that Lovage continued to be cultivated and esteemed through the Dark Ages, as it is among the sixteen herbs that were listed in a plan which survives of a 9th-century physic garden belonging to the Benedictine monastery at St. Gall, in Switzerland.

Thomas Tusser, in his *Five Hundred Pointes of Good Husbandrie* (1573), gave Lovage with his particular plants which were "Necessary Herbs to grow in the garden of Physic." The old writers recommended an infusion of Lovage roots for relieving gravel, jaundice and kidney troubles, but Culpepper, who had uses for all parts of the plant, thought the seeds most powerful for certain treatments. He wrote of Lovage: "It is an herb of the Sun in Taurus, if Saturn offend the throat—as he always does, if he be occasioner of the malady, and Taurus is the genesis —this is your cure." This apothecary also advised the ancient use of the distilled water of Lovage for helping pleurisy patients and to be used as a gargle and mouthwash for comforting those with quinsy, and he maintained that: "Being dropped into the eyes it taketh away redness or dimness of them; it likewise taketh away spots or freckles in the face." As a poultice he prescribed: "The leaves bruised and fried with a little hog's lard and laid hot to any blotch or boil will quickly break it."

Lovage is a hardy perennial with thick, erect stems reaching five feet or more in height. The large radical leaves are divided into narrow wedge-like "leaflets" resembling those of coarse Celery. As an umbelliferous plant, it bears umbels of Fennel-like yellow flowers. Its Latin name, *Ligusticum levisticum*, is said to have originated from Liguria, an Italian province where these plants grew in abundance. This herb is easy to grow in a sunny bed of well-drained soil that is rich in humus. New plants may be propagated from root-offsets or divisions, in early spring, or they may be raised from seed sown preferably in late summer when just ripe. When given the chance, Lovage sows its own seeds very satisfactorily.

MARIGOLD

"The Marigold that goes to bed wi' th' sun, and with him rises weeping," says Perdita in Shakespeare's *The Winter's Tale*. The Marigold was always associated with the sun and believed to look only in his direction, opening its flowers on his rising, to close them as he set. The Romans found this plant was usually in bloom on the first day of each month, the calends, and this is the reason for its Latin generic name, *Calendula*. Its specific name *officinalis*, of the herbal shops, was given to all official medicinal herbs. Long ago the Marigold was known as "Mary Gowles," or by the older poets, as "Mary Golde."

Marigolds were considered particularly effective for restoring eyes to health. One famous herbalist said that only to look on Marigolds would draw evil humours out of the head and strengthen the eyes. Another ancient recommended the Marigold as a method of detection, saying: "It must be taken only when the moon is in the sign of the Virgin and not when Jupiter is in the ascendant, for then the herb loses its virtue. And the gatherer, who must be out of deadly sin, must say three Pater Nosters and three Aves. It will give the wearer a vision of anyone who has robbed him."

Only the deep-orange-flowered Marigold possessed the curative virtues for which the plant was prescribed. The prescription for King Henry VIII's own "Medycine for the Pestilence" read: "Take a handfull of Marigolds, a handful of sorel, and a handful of burnet, half a handful of fetterfew, half a handful of rew." There followed a further ingredient "draggons" (Snapdragons), then the method of seething, and finally, the hope that "if yt be taken before that pimpulls do apere yt will hele the syke person with God's Grace."

This plant was at one time associated with the Virgin Mary, and it was the emblem of Queen Mary:

> "To Mary our queen, that flower so sweet,
>   This marigold I do apply;"

was part of a ballad of her time.

In the 17th century Culpepper included in his list of Marigold's uses: "They strengthen the heart exceedingly, and are very expulsive, and a little less effectual in the smallpox and measles than saffron. The juice of Marigold leaves mixed with vinegar, and any hot swelling bathed with it, instantly gives ease, and assuages it. The flowers, either green or dried, are much used in possets, broths, and drink, as a comforter of the heart and spirits, and to expel any malignant or pestilential quality which might annoy them." He described a Marigold "plaister" made, with the powdered dried flowers mixed with lard, turpentine and rosin,

Marigold

to be placed on the breast to "succour" the heart and ease any kind of fever.

In his *Antheologie* (1655) Fuller wrote to the Marigold: "We all know the many and sovereign virtues in your leaves (petals), the Herbe Generalle in all pottage." And in *Maison Rustique* or *The Countrie Farme* (1699) Stevens gives the Marigold as a remedy for headaches, toothache, jaundice, red eyes and ague. He also said that a "conserve made of the flowers and sugar, taken in the morning fasting, cureth the trembling of the harte, and is also given in the time of plague or pestilence." This author gave some idea of the demand for the herb in his day: "The yellow leaves (petals) of the flowers are dried and kept throughout Dutchland against winter to put into broths, physicall potions and for divers other purposes, in such quantity that in some Grocers or spice-sellers are to be found barrels filled with them and retailed by the penny or less, insomuch that no broths are well made without dried Marigold."

As a culinary herb Marigold gave its tangy flavour to broths, soups, stews, porridge, etc., and the leaves and petals were considered excellent in salads. In a stillroom account of Tudor times, "Marigold Water" is mentioned. One critical old herbalist said he had learned that some use Marygold flowers to make their hair yellow, not being content with the natural colour God gave them. A yellow dye extracted from the flowers by boiling was used for other purposes apart from tinting hair.

This Marigold, Pot Marigold as it is called, is a native of Southern Europe. Its Daisy flowers place it in the Daisy group, *Compositae*. It is an annual to grow from seed. Once these plants have flowered and seeded in a garden they reappear each year blooming until frost-bitten.

MARJORAM

Marjoram's own particular scent and flavour made it famous at an early date. It went into Greek and Roman food and perfumes, and had a high reputation as a medicine. The Greeks used it internally as an antidote for narcotic poisons, for convulsions, and to relieve dropsical cases. Externally, it was valued for fomentations. Marjoram's proper name *Origanum*, from two Greek words *oros*, mountain, and *ganos*, brightness, not only derived from its delightful scent and appearance when blossoming on the hillsides, but from its use as the herb of happiness with which the Greeks and the Romans crowned their young lovers. Their dead, too, were considered to be blissful if Marjoram grew on their graves.

There are several varieties of Marjoram for culinary uses including the wild type, *O. vulgare*, that is quite common on the English chalk downs and is familiarly known as "Organ" or "Organy," and this became "Bastard Marjoram" after the introduction of the less hardy foreign types. Gerard said it was "exceedingly well knowne to all" and he maintained that among its virtues "it is very good against the warmbling of the stomach, and stayeth the desire to vomit, especially at sea." This was the kind most used for medicine, being the popular cure for earache, coughs, bladder disorders, dropsy, etc. Culpepper said: "Our common Sweet Marjoram is warming and comfortable in cold diseases of the head, stomach, sinews and other parts taken inwardly or outwardly applied," and he continued with a list of other comforts it supplied that must have covered most human ailments. Marjoram tea was so popular a remedy that the plant was taken to New England by the settlers where it became naturalized and common in the eastern states of America.

Marjoram is entirely aromatic, with a strong peculiar fragrance and taste which is retained when dried so that it was esteemed both as a culinary herb and a scent, being strewn in chambers, made into "Sweet bags," "Sweet Powders" and "Sweet Washing Waters." It was also used to scour furniture. There was once a belief that sprays of Marjoram and Wild Thyme laid by milk in a dairy prevented its being curdled by thunder. The plant provided a rather dull purple dye for wool and a reddish-brown one for linen, but it was fleeting and of little value save for peasants who wove their own cloths. Marjoram was employed in brewing ale before the introduction of hops, and continued to be liked as an aromatic flavour and preservative in beer.

The French Marjoram, *O. onites*, Pot Marjoram, a native of southern Europe, is the most useful kind to grow in a herb garden for culinary use, being more aromatic and of a stronger and more delicious flavour than the British wild type. It was used here long before the plants were introduced into English gardens. It is a hardy perennial about a foot high, with lush bright green leaves and purplish-pink flower-heads.

The Portuguese and North African Marjoram, *O. marjorana*, is the Oregano of recipes, or Knotted Marjoram as it is called because of the grey-green bracts, like knots holding the flowers. Its scented foliage is greyish and of a delicious flavour and it is rightly named the "Sweet Marjoram." This sort is only half-hardy and needs to be grown in a cool greenhouse or tried as a long-lasting pot plant indoors as it was grown many centuries ago. This is the "Sweet Margerome," Gerard's herb of

Marjoram

"marvellous sweet smell," of which Parkinson also wrote, "to please outward senses in nosegays and in windows of houses." When grown in a garden it must be treated as a half-hardy annual raised from seed sown under glass in March and planted outside in June.

The Winter Marjoram, *O. heracleoticum*, comes from Greece, but is hardy enough to grow outside in Britain so long as it is given a reasonably sheltered bed of dryish soil that does not become waterlogged in winter.

The Marjorams belong to the Labiatae family. In Greek mythology many plants were supposed to arise from the changing of a person into a plant. Marjoram is said to have been first called Amarakos, or Amaracon, from Amaracus a Greek youth in the service of Cinyres, King of Cyprus. He accidentally broke a vase of perfume and, terrified, he fell to the ground unconscious, but was mercifully changed by the gods into this herb which bore his name. This through the centuries became Majorana and eventually Marjoram.

MINT

"The smell of Mint does stir up the minde and the taste to a greedy desire of meat," so, according to Gerard, wrote Pliny of this appetizing Mediterranean herb. It was always important to everyone and wherever civilization spread Mint went along with it and established itself where it was happy. It was taken to America by the Pilgrim Fathers, where in some congenial situations it has now become an unwelcome weed.

The Greeks and Romans used Mint as a bath-scent, and the Athenians, who scented every part of the body with particular herbs, used Mint for the arms as the smell of strength. It was used to flavour all kinds of food and drinks (Mint sauce was a Roman inspiration) and it provided medicine for numerous disorders. Tables were scoured with it in preparation for feasting, floors were strewn with it so that guests treading on it were stimulated by the odour.

The Romans brought Mint to grow in Britain where it remained the most popular of herbs. It was listed as being cultivated in monastic gardens in the 9th century, and it is interesting that in the Middle Ages it was used to whiten teeth as it is still employed in toothpastes today. Turner in his *Herball*, compiled in 1568, calls garden Mint "Spere Mynte." In the 17th century Culpepper named nearly forty ailments

Mint

which could be treated with Mint, including an effective hair-wash for heads inclined to sores.

Mint is a member of the Labiatae family, and the generic name *Mentha* is of mythological origin, and was first given by Theophrastus. Menthe was a nymph beloved by Pluto, and the jealous Proserpine changed her into this plant.

Apart from the usual "Pea" and "Lamb" Mint, there are several types of the genus which should also be grown for kitchen use. And there are other kinds of Mint that cover stones and spread carpets on paving or make fragrant little "lawns" that are a pleasure to tread upon. Chaucer refers to "a little path of mintes full and fenill green."

The best culinary Mints are *Mentha viridis*, the well-known Spearmint, Lamb Mint, Pea Mint; *M. rotundifolia*, Apple Mint, which grows three feet tall with pale green leaves that taste and smell of russet apples. Its variety *M. r. variegata*, is an attractive plant with its foliage splashed with cream and white, but best of all is the hybrid *M. r.* variety Bowles, with pale green woolly leaves of a rather apple-like flavour borne on stems reaching five feet high. This is the connoisseurs' type, it makes delicious Mint sauce used either alone or in equal parts with Lamb Mint. It dries well and keeps its soft grey-green colour. *M. rubra raripila*, is a lesser-known Mint, but its good qualities recommend it. Its smooth leaves on purple stems have the true Lamb Mint flavour and it is free from rust, the disease that is the curse of most Mints. *M. citrata*, Eau de Cologne Mint, a variety of the Chartreuse, has leaves tinged with bronze-purple, purple stems and runners, and a delightful fragrance for sachets and a pleasant taste in orange jelly. Its sister the Pineapple Mint, with a fruitier flavour that is a mixture of pineapple and lemon, is also good for flavouring lemon or orange jellies.

The creeping Mints for paving and carpeting are the white-flowered *M. gattefossei*, and the extraordinary *M. requienii*, the tiniest flowering plant grown in Britain, being only half an inch high with blossoms no bigger than a pin-head, but it has a sturdy Minty scent. Where it is suited, it grows into a velvet mat. It prefers a warm sheltered, dampish bed in which to flourish.

To keep culinary Mints in perfect flavour, they must be well fed with compost, and where possible they should be shifted to a new bed or have their old one enriched with compost every two years. They are not fussy about situation so long as they are not too dry in summer or waterlogged in winter; they give their best in a well-drained bed with plenty of humus in the soil.

Mint rust is a fungus disease that causes swollen stems and orange-coloured patches followed by dark brown powdery pustules on stem and leaf. There is no cure for it, and the infected plants must be burnt, the ground should be cleaned with quicklime, and the new Mint plants must be grown in a fresh place.

WATER CRESS AND NASTURTIUM

The ancient Greeks believed Water Cress was especially beneficial for sharpening the intellect and had a popular saying: "Eat Cress and learn more wit." The Persians were instructed to give Water Cress to their children to make them grow, and it does possess real medicinal virtues which are anti-scorbutic, blood enriching, stimulating to the digestion and entirely health-giving.

Water Cress was cultivated commercially on the Continent so long ago as the middle of the 16th century by Nicholas Mesner of Erfurt. Then beds were laid in Holland and Germany, but Britain still relied on its wild supplies until nearly a hundred years later, when an enterprising Mr. Bradbury started a Water Cress farm. From an early date "Water Creses" were hawked in city streets for use in salads, soups, etc., and at all times the herb was prescribed by physicians and apothecaries for various illnesses. Culpepper recommended Water Cress "pottage" to cleanse the blood in spring and "consume the gross humour Winter hath left behind; those that would live in health may use it if they please, if they will not I cannot help it. If any fancy not the pottage, they may eat the herb as a salad." He also praised its other curative uses, then said: "The leaves bruised or the juice, is good to be applied to the face or other parts troubled with freckles, pimples, spots or the like, at night, and washed away in the morning." This advice was given when skin diseases were common distresses, for no vegetables were available out of season and salted meat was winter's diet.

Water Cress's botanical name *Nasturtium officinalis*, was derived from *nasus tortus*, a convulsed nose, from the supposed effect of the plant's pungent taste. It is of the Cabbage family Cruciferae, of which all members bear flowers with four petals like a cross; all are beneficial.

There are several kinds of Cress which have the same wholesomeness as the Water type and are good anti-scorbutic herbs. The American Land

Nasturtium

Water Cress

Cress or Winter Cress, *Barbarea*, dedicated to Saint Barbara, can be grown in any good moisture-holding soil in a partly shaded bed. It is a perennial with a similar flavour to Water Cress. The tiny Cress usually associated with Mustard, by name *Lepidium sativum*, may be grown on the surface of the soil in the garden, where the seeds should be watered and covered until they germinate. Or it can be grown in shallow boxes or containers indoors. The seedlings are ready to cut when an inch high.

Any gardener who is lucky enough to have a spring or stream available can grow Water Cress, and the inventive gardener may make a suitable shallow gravelly bed if a trickle of water from a tap can be arranged through a plastic pipe buried under the soil. Water Cress has an iron content and should be grown in some shade to keep green, as if exposed to the sun the leaves turn brown.

The Nasturtium's sharp taste was its only connection with the true Nasturtium, the homely Water Cress. The brilliant-flowered exotic annual was properly called *Tropaeolum*, and its popular name, Indian Cress, referred to the Peruvian Indians. It grew wild in the Inca's gold-laden land that was ravished by the Spaniards, who frequently lost their rich booty to adventuring Englishmen, awaiting their homeward-bound galleons. And it is interesting that the *Tropaeolum* was brought to English gardens in 1596, during this desperate period of treasure-seeking.

The name *Tropaeolum*, came from the Latin *tropaeum*, a trophy (as displayed after victory by Greeks and Romans), and was an imaginative reference to the helmet-shaped flowers and shield-like leaves. This Nasturtium and its varieties solely represent their own family Tropaeolacae. The leaves taste like Water Cress and are beneficial and good in salad and for other purposes. The seeds make excellent imitation Capers, and the bright edible flowers are splendidly decorative for several dishes.

One first-class herb farm grows masses of Nasturtiums not only for use but around apple trees as a preventative against certain pests, which they find are deterred by this plant.

PARSLEY

Parsley is Britain's commonest culinary herb, but like most others it is generally ill-used and its possibilities are neglected. Its pretty sprays which garnish many dishes are set aside when they should be eaten, as they are probably more health-giving than the dish they adorn. Small quantities of its finely-chopped leaves are allowed to bespeckle white sauce for fish and other things, and a few Parsley leaves have been placed in salads by venturesome cooks, to be carefully removed by unadventurous diners.

Parsley may be poisonous to birds and lethal to the parrot tribe, but it is completely beneficial to man and to other animals who sense what is good for them. For instance, hares and rabbits seek it and eat it avidly, sheep like it because if they can eat enough it prevents foot-rot. Parsley's benefits should be equally appreciated by people. It is as rich a source of Vitamin A as most grades of Cod Liver oil, and is richer in Vitamin C than any other food, containing at least three times as much as oranges. Parsley's valuable constituent, Apiol, was discovered in 1849 and is of great service in the treatment of malarial disorders and other maladies. The ancients knew this herb's value for treating rheumatic patients, and Parsley tea was a common remedy for that distress and others, particularly those of the kidneys, and it was prescribed for dropsy and jaundice. It was also a gentle stimulant; and as a relief for flatulence it used to be given like Dill water, to fretful infants with wind.

The appreciation of Parsley began in the distant past, when the ancient Greeks reverenced the herb as having sprung from the blood of their mythological hero Archemorus, the forerunner of death, who was carelessly laid by his nurse on a Parsley leaf and was eaten by serpents. This superstitious connection with death led to their popular saying, "to be in need of Parsley" which meant to be hopelessly ill. Plutarch described an occurrence when a Greek army on the march met some donkeys loaded with Parsley and panicked with foreboding. As it was the herb of oblivion, the Greeks made Parsley wreaths for the tombs of their dead.

And they had happier uses for Parsley. Homer said the warriors fed their chariot horses with the leaves. It was a Grecian custom to crown the victors of the Isthmian games with Parsley chaplets; they were also worn for certain feasts as Theocritus described:

> "At Sparta's Palace twenty beauteous mayds
> The pride of Greece, fresh garlands crowned their heads
> With hyacinths and twining parsley drest
> Graced joyful Menelaus' marriage feast."

Parsley

The beds in Grecian gardens were often planted with thick borders of Parsley and Rue.

Parsley, being very closely related to Caraway shares the generic name *Carum*, but its specific name *Petroselinum*, rock Parsley, comes from the Greek name *petroselinon* given by Dioscorides. In the Middle Ages this was corrupted into *Petrocilium*, which became in England Petersylinge, then Persele and Persely and finally Parsley. The herb was first dedicated to Persephone, and later by the Christians to St. Peter when he succeeded Charon as the guide to the souls of the dead.

The date of Parsley's introduction into British gardens appears to be uncertain. Probably the Romans brought it as they had numerous uses for the herb and grew several varieties, and Pliny actually mentioned the *crispum* sort. But some authorities believe it arrived in 1548, although according to ancient writings it was already familiar here in Tudor times. "Water of Parcelly" was among the usual still-room products listed in a household book of that period. And in 1551 William Turner wrote: "If Parsley is thrown into fish-ponds it will heal the sick fishes therein." Nicholas Culpepper believed Parsley to be an effective remedy for much suffering and of some uses he said: "It is very comfortable to the stomach . . . and to break wind in the stomach and bowels . . . and openeth obstructions both of the liver and spleen . . . The seed is effectual to break the stone and to ease the pains and torment thereof."

Parsley is a hardy umbelliferous biennial and new seed should be sown (shallowly) each year in April and August for a useful succession. The seedlings must be thinned out when an inch high. A well-drained, fairly rich soil is required to grow the best plants, and if the flower-stems and coarse leaves are removed in summer and the plants are watered, a new crop of tender foliage will soon grow.

POPPY

There are two kinds of Poppy that should be grown in herb gardens for the sake of their beautiful flowers and their tasty seeds. The Oriental Poppy is the perennial and the Opium Poppy the annual type. The scarlet *Papaver orientale* originated as a wild plant in Asia Minor, brilliantly enriching the countryside of Armenia and the Caucasus. Its giant blooms are unsurpassed by any other garden flower; their great, crêpe silk petals surround a central boss of stigmas arranged like the spokes of a wheel set amid masses of indigo stamens. All Poppy stigmas are interesting, as they form a mechanical projecting roof to the round ovary or capsule. This protects the loose seeds from rain. Just below the roof there are perforations that in wet weather are closed with little flaps, but at the right time they act like a pepper-pot for scattering the ripe seeds.

This flamboyant Poppy was cultivated for many centuries in the gardens of the East and West, but the later Victorians regarded it as spoiling "everything of a quiet refined nature that happens to be in the vicinity." They thought the plant more fitting for public grounds or distant vistas, whereas this Poppy's flowers should be enjoyed closely and may be taken indoors, where they will live in water for several days. For this pleasure, the buds should be cut just as the two green boat-shaped sepals part to disclose the packed crumpled petals. It is wonderful to watch the magnificent bloom unfold from so small and creased a parcel.

Oriental Poppies certainly have disadvantages as garden plants, because they bloom early in June and only for a very short season, after which the foliage appears exhausted and dies for a while. But the brief display is so satisfying that space should be found for the plants where their languishing leaves may be hidden by the summer growth of other things. Also, they flop with the weight of bud and bloom especially when moisture is lacking, and to cope with this failing a few supporting pea-sticks need to be placed among them at an early stage.

The scarlet type has been developed into various coloured hybrids ranging from rich mahogany, bright cerise, crimson, blood-red, orange-scarlet, golden-orange and salmon-pink to a white-flowered form with a rich blue blotch at the base of the petals. There are double-flowered ones but in them the characteristic design of the single flower's centre is lost.

The Opium Poppy of ancient gardens has smooth grey-green leaves, and its flowers are smaller than *Orientale*'s; they may be double or single, fringed or plain, in colours varying from white through all shades of red and purple to nearly blue. This is the Grecian wild Poppy which is found in most parts of Asia Minor. It is *Papaver somniferum*, the sleep-inducing one and the reliever of pain. Its milky blood is opium, which gives morphine, codein and other valuable drugs, but only from plants grown in the East, those reared in Europe have a poor yield. The medicinal virtues of this Poppy were discovered in earliest times, for there is evidence of their cultivation by Neolithic man, who would at

Opium Poppy

least have something to ease his discomforts. The Greek, Roman and Arabian physicians used this blissful herb, and it was always an important crop in monastic physic gardens, then in domestic ones. The large seed-heads were kept for poulticing and medicines. The seeds contained no trace of morphine, only a pale yellow fixed oil useful to artists and others, but they had a delicious nutty taste and were used to flavour bread and cakes, and to provide pet birds with "Mawseed."

The origin of the name *Papaver* is too doubtful for botanists to explain with certainty; some suggest the plant's comforting juice was put into pre-historic, fretful babies' supper milk, which in Celtic was called *papa:* others, less imaginative, say it is "Latin and obscure."

The ancient Greeks dedicated the Poppy to Aphrodite, the golden-haired goddess in charge of vegetation; the Romans claimed it as the flower of Ceres, who had much the same duties and was always portrayed carrying Poppies and corn in the hand not occupied with a flaming torch. Poppies have no nectar but are attractive to bees who collect the pollen to make into "bee bread."

Poppies like a place in the sun in well-drained soil. The perennial should be planted in autumn and given a mulch of compost each spring.

ROSE

The Rose has been the most beautiful and exploited of useful herbs since early man found it was good to eat, drink and smell; to wash and perfume his body; to ease many maladies; and it was good to meditate upon; to wear and to offer in homage to earthly and spiritual love. He dedicated it to his lovers and his gods, and entirely enjoyed it.

The cultivated Rose was born in Persia and taken through Palestine and Asia Minor to the Greeks. They dedicated it to Aphrodite and planted it in their colonies in Southern Italy, to be grown as a crop to satisfy the constantly increasing uses they found for it. Demands from the prosperous elegants, especially of Sybaris, were insatiable, their beds were daily made deep with fresh petals, their floors and couches were strewn with them and petals lay on their tables set for feasting. They made salads and wine, perfumes and unguents from them. Paestum, ancient Poseidonia, became the Rose city, and its device was a syren holding a Rose. From the sale of Roses its beautiful buildings were erected, around whose ruins now Roses remain still faithful.

Rose

Homer wrote of Roses, so did Sappho, 600 B.C. The name was from the Greek word for red, *rhodon*, because the ancient blooms were the deep crimson ones of *Rosa gallica*, with the headiest perfume.

The rich Romans, experts of pleasure, made the Rose its symbol. They devoured shiploads of Roses from Egypt, and, as the Sybarites had done, they slept, walked and fed on them. They made Rose conserves and sweetmeats and dropped their petals in wine-cups to delay drunkenness, and as a further precaution they wore Rose garlands when feasting. Rose wine was enjoyed as were Rose perfumes. Roman brides and bridegrooms wore Rose crowns, like all the numerous statues of Cupid, Venus and Bacchus. And Roman heroes, the victors, were given chaplets of Roses and walked or rode their chariots on Rose-strewn paths. When a white Rose, the emblem of honour, secrecy and silence, was hung above banqueting tables, it was understood that all guests could speak and act with confidence in the knowledge that everyone present was bound to secrecy. From this custom came not only the term *sub rosa*, privately, but the "rose," the plaster ornament in the centre of a ceiling.

Both Horace and Pliny wrote at length on the culture of Roses, and new varieties were evolved. The demand for these flowers was so insistent that to force them out of season vast networks of heating-pipes were laid down in nurseries.

For the Romans, Roses were the flower of Venus, born from sea-foam, and in her honour they decorated the prows of their warships with Rose garlands. The use of Roses was not entirely gay and voluptuous; physicians employed them for their Rose-hip and Rose-petal syrups, for plasters, electuaries, and other aids for patients with heart, stomach, liver or chest troubles. And Rose wreaths were made for funerals. Eventually, Venus's flower of love was consecrated by the Christians to Our Lady and became a spiritual guard against witchcraft and all evil.

The ancient Rose perfumes such as *Oleum rosarum* were made of a fatty oil scented with Rose petals; the first distilled Rose-water was invented by Avicenna in the 10th century.

The Crusaders were often credited with bringing the Eastern Rose, and the name, back from Damascus to Western Europe, but as the type was known in France for many centuries before Crusades were thought of it must have been brought by the earliest pilgrims returning from the Holy Land.

In the 14th century Edward I adopted the Rose as the emblem of

England where it had long been used for food, medicines and pleasure and was cultivated in all gardens.

Red-flowered Roses are the choice for herb gardens as they have the strongest scent and flavour, with acknowledged medicinal virtues. The best kinds are the lovely ancient Apothecary's Rose, *R. gallica*; the Old Cabbage Rose, *R. centifolia*; and the deep pink Damask Rose, *R. damascena*. French perfume-distillers in the Grasse districts, whose business is odour, also use some more modern varieties such as Rose de Hai, Mrs. John Laing and Caroline Testout.

When the old-fashioned Roses are deeply planted in good soil they often spread into large clumps. They should be pruned after flowering as, unlike newer hybrids, they bloom on the previous year's shoots.

ROSEMARY

The symbolism associated with Rosemary gave it a special place among herbs. Sir Thomas More wrote: "As for Rosmarine. I lett it runne all over my garden walls, not onlie because my bees love it, but because it is the herb sacred to remembrance, and, therefore, to friendship; whence a sprig of it hath a dumb language that maketh it the chosen emblem of our funeral wakes and in our buriall grounds."

Rosemary was endowed with mystical powers strong enough to guard the church, the dead and the living from all evil. It was grown in churchyards, and its boughs were kept inside churches and were also burnt as incense, *incensier* being an old French name for it. It was a necessity in gardens. Herrick said of *The Rosemary Branch:*

> "Grow for two ends, it matters not at all,
> Be't for my bridal or my burial."

At funerals a sprig of Rosemary was given to each mourner on leaving the house, to be carried until the burial when it was dropped on the coffin. For weddings, as the herb of fidelity, Rosemary dipped in scented water was woven into the bride's chaplet. The guests were presented with its gilded branches tied with silk ribbons of various colours, as emblems of love and loyalty.

In his sermon "A Marriage Present," published in 1607, the celebrated Reverend Roger Hacket said: "Speaking of the powers of rosemary, it overtoppeth all the flowers in the garden, boasting man's rule. It helpeth the brain, strengtheneth the memories, and is very medicinable for the head. Another property of the rosemary is, it affects the heart. Let this rosmarinus, this flower of men, ensigne of your wisdom, love and loyaltie, be carried not only in your hands, but in your hearts and heads."

A few chopped Rosemary leaves were added to wedding cakes as to Christmas puddings and other festive fare. And the boughs were of significance in Christmas decorations, as Herrick described in his *Ceremony Upon Candlemas Eve:*

> "Down with the rosemary and so
> Down with the bays and mistletoe;
> Down with the holly, ivy, all,
> Wherewith ye dressed the Christmas Hall:
> That so the superstitious find
> No one least branch there left behind."

This cordial herb was used to flavour wine and ale and became an ingredient of Eau de Cologne.

Rosemary's natural home was in southern Europe where its many excellent qualities were always valued, its scent and flavour were enjoyed, and its superstitious and medicinal uses were many, Roman and Arabian physicians regarding it as particularly effective for restoring speech after a stroke.

The plant was generally believed to have been introduced into England in 1548, but an old tradition held that during the Black Death, in the 14th century Queen Phillipa's mother, the Countess of Hainault, sent her supplies of Rosemary branches as a protection against the plague. For a long time it had the reputation of being an effectual disinfectant and, like Rue, was in the bunches of aromatic herbs taken into courts as a protection against jail-fever. It was also burnt in sick rooms and hospitals.

Considerable use was made of Rosemary by the old physicians. It was given for complaints of the chest; as a stimulant against depression; an aid to digestion; for liver ailments; for diseases of the brain and for gout. Hungary water was long famous. This was invented for Elizabeth Queen of Hungary, 1235, and was made from Rosemary in spirits of wine; it was applied outwardly and said to have completely cured her paralysed limbs. Rosemary's burnt wood was rubbed on teeth to preserve them, and bread baked on it was prescribed to restore the loss of "smellynge." The author of *Banckes' Herbal* said: "Make thee

Rosemary

a box of the wood of rosemary and smell it and it shall preserve thy youth."

The growth of this beautiful evergreen shrub according to an old belief, was symbolic of Christ's life on earth. For thirty-three years it grew in height reaching just over six feet, then increased only in breadth. It was also associated with the Virgin Mary in many legends.

Rosemary grew wild on the sea-cliffs and its name *Rosmarinus* meant sea-spray. It belongs to the Labiatae family and is entirely aromatic with a scent rather like old-fashioned ginger-beer. The type's dusky leaves are silvered underneath and its soft blue flowers are borne in spring. The shrub is inclined to grow straggly and needs a light cutting after it has flowered. It may be planted as a thick, low hedge which must be trimmed immediately after blossoming. The variety Miss Jessop, grows upright and compact, but is less hardy; its foliage is a yellower green and the flowers are paler than the original.

Rosemary grows best in a light, well-drained soil in a sheltered position, preferably at the base of a south wall. It looks aged and romantic when trained against a wall as it may be seen at Sissinghurst Castle and in other old gardens. It is said to be more fragrant when grown on chalky soil, but then the bush grows much smaller.

RUE

According to Pliny, Rue was eaten in great quantities by artists of his day. It was credited not only with preserving sight, sharpening vision and easing strained eyes, but also with giving second sight. The Greeks, too, regarded it as a mystical herb and a powerful protection against magic spells and enchantments; to mention one instance, it relieved the nervous indigestion which often attacked the shy ones when dining out among strangers, and this trouble was seriously attributed to the evil-wishing or witchcraft of some ill-disposed fellow guest.

Rue was an extremely versatile medicinal herb, being used in a great variety of treatments. It was prescribed for at least eighty-four different ailments in Pliny's day. The great Hippocrates gave it special attention and recommendation, and the herb's generic name *Ruta*, derived from a Greek word meaning "to set free," was given because of its releasing action in many maladies and distresses. It was the main ingredient in the famous poison antidote of the amazing toxicologist Eupator Mithridates VI, king of Pontus A.D. 120–63. He personally experimented with

Rue

poisons and their antidotes so long and so assiduously that it is said that after annexing Roman territory and causing three wars, when he was finally defeated by Pompey, he vainly tried to poison himself, but found he had become immune and persuaded a slave to stab him.

As a poison antidote, Rue's reputation persisted through many centuries and Gerard wrote: "If a man be anointed with the juice of rue, the poison of wolf's bane, mushrooms, or todestooles, the biting of serpents, stinging of scorpions, spiders, bees, hornets and wasps will not hurt him."

The Romans introduced Rue and their estimation of its qualities into Britain, and it became one of the most cherished of old English garden plants, commonly grown for domestic medical remedies and for its continued use as a mystical, protective herb not only for defeating ill luck from witches and evil, but also as a disinfectant against contagion, especially from the dreaded and often recurring plague. In the 18th century it became one of the ingredients, like Garlic, of the effective Four Thieves' "Vinegar." Rue was for ages an important inclusion in the bunches of aromatic herbs carried by judges into court as a safeguard against the infection of the typhus fever suffered by prisoners. It was also strewn in the courts, and sprigs of it were placed on the dock benches. Gerard's recipe for a disinfecting paste was: "The leaves of Rue eaten with the kernels of Walnuts or figs stamped together and made into a masse or paste, is good against all eville aires, the pestilence or plague."

Rue was a holy and purifying herb, popularly called Herbygrass, and brushes made from it were at one time used to sprinkle the holy water at the ceremony preceding High Mass on Sundays. It was the Herb of Repentance, and Shakespeare several times referred to it; in Hamlet it was in Ophelia's sad little posy: "There's rue for you; and here's some for me; we may call it herb of grace o' Sundays"; and in Richard III: "Here in this place I'll set a bank of rue, sour herb of grace; Rue even for ruth, shall shortly here be seen, the remembrance of a weeping queen."

Culpepper in the 17th century advised Rue for sciatica and pains in the joints, if the latter be "anointed" with it, as also for "the shaking fits of agues, to take a draught before the fit comes." He had curious prescriptions for comforting earache and aiding dim sight: "The juice thereof warmed in a pomegranate shell or rind, and dropped into ears, helps the pains of them. The juice of it and fennel, with a little honey, and the gall

of a cock put thereunto, helps dimness of the eyesight". Milton's Angel
purged Adam's sight with "Euphrasy and Rue."

Rue is a beautiful and hardy little shrubby plant about three feet tall,
of the citrus fruit family Rutaceae. It is a native of Southern Europe but
quite hardy in Britain. Rue is evergreen, or "evergrey," as the finely-cut
leaves are pale sea-green and powdered with white bloom; the small
flowers have bright yellow petals surrounding an emerald centre. The
plant is entirely aromatic and has a coconut-like scent rather resembling
that of Gorse blossom. Its culinary uses are limited, but a few finely-
chopped leaves may be used Italian fashion, to add zest to a salad or to
make appetizing sandwiches.

SAGE

"Why should a man die whilst sage grows in his garden?" expressed
the Latin opinion of the grey-leaved aromatic little shrub, "Sage the
saviour." The name of the genus, *Salvia*, was derived from the Latin
salvus, well, healthy, and this Mediterranean native supplied remedies
for illness and flavours for food and it whitened teeth.

Reading the long lists of ailments that down the centuries were
treated with Sage, it appears that the ancients had few maladies for
which this herb was not prescribed. Dioscorides claimed it the remedy
for most kidney troubles, and while curing them, he said, it turned faded
hair black. He advised it for ulcers, for rheumatism, consumption,
coughs, sore throats and almost any other distress. Pliny was of the
opinion that it also cured serpent bites; and Culpepper included in his
list of benefits: "Sage is of excellent use to help the memory, warming
and quickening the senses." He recorded its value in times of plague.
Gerard described several varieties of Sage growing in his garden at
Holborn, affirmed all the known uses of Sage and praised the wholesomeness of Sage Ale.

Another old belief in Sage's powers was that it alleviated grief. This
was strongly held in parts of France, and Pepys wrote in his diary:
"Between Gosport and Southampton we observed a little churchyard
where it was customary to sow all the graves with Sage." Sage plants
were so valuable that it was once the custom to plant Rue near them to
guard them from "noxious" toads.

Sage grows wild along the northern shores of the Mediterranean from
Spain to the Adriatic; the best kind flourishes on the islands near

Fiume, and there, since Greece was great, has been made the most flavoursome Sage honey, an ancient expensive luxury. Sage tea was always popular, and it is said that when it reached the Chinese they preferred the brew to their native tea, and exchanged with the Dutch three times the amount of their choicest varieties for Sage.

Many Italian and other country people still eat Sage "to be healthy," making sandwiches of the leaves between bread and butter. One of the oldest culinary uses for this wonderful herb is for flavouring cheese, and its digestive qualities have secured its popular acceptance as the perfect accompaniment of such rich fare as duck, pork and goose. And pork sausages used to be made more tasty and digestible when flavoured with Sage.

The Salvias belong to the Labiatae family, of which square stems are a characteristic feature. Of the many varieties of Salvias, the culinary ones are the most important for the small herb garden, but where space permits some others should be included for the sake of their foliage and bloom-spikes. Of the culinary kinds, Garden Sage, *S. officinalis*, is the commonest and its Broad-Leaved variety, which seldom flowers, has the most pungent flavour in its large grey-green leaves. Red Sage, the purple-leaved variety, and Golden Sage, with yellow streaked foliage, are both decorative and well flavoured. The Red variegated variety, bearing purple flowers, is the "Painted Sage" described by Parkinson in his *Garden of Pleasure* as having leaves "diversely marked and spotted with white and red among the greene." This attractive plant has the habit of reverting to plain green and may be renewed each year from rooted cuttings. The delicious Pineapple Sage, *S. rutilans*, with true pineapple scent and flavour, is only half-hardy and must be taken indoors before winter. It can be tried as a pot-plant on a sunny windowsill, where its scarlet flowers would be an autumn pleasure.

Some of the decorative perennial Sages are the grey hairy-leaved type, *S. azurea*, with four-feet-high spikes of vivid blue blossoms; the Brazilian Sage, *S. uliginosa*, a swamp Sage, which bears bright blue flowers on stems five feet tall, and likes a moisture-holding soil; and Violet Sage, *S. virgata nemerosa*, which makes a branching plant with long bloom-sprays of purple bracts and violet-blue flowers. It reaches about three feet high.

Sages appreciate good rich lightish soil in a bed sheltered from winter winds. The culinary sorts easily root when branches are pegged down into soil, or they may be grown from cuttings. It is advisable to make

Sage

new plants to replace old ones of three years' growth, as these become straggly and woody and deteriorate in flavour.

SAVORY

Summer Savory and Winter Savory are the only two types out of fourteen species of this fragrant genus that will live with any zest in Britain. Other members of this Mediterranean group have been tempted but without much success. Summer Savory is an annual and the Winter kind is a hardy perennial. These plants, on the authority of the ancients, belong to the Satyrs, and they would surely make handsome crowns for the wanton woodland deities. They resemble large-leaved Thyme or, perhaps, Rosemary, with rich dark green leaves, whose warm aromatic scent and taste is so spicy that they were highly prized for culinary flavourings long before spices came from the East. Virgil classed them among the most fragrant of sweet herbs and advised their planting near bee-hives to give an especially attractive taste to the honey. Pliny called the Savorys *Satureia*, their old Latin name, and that remained the botanical title of the genus. The ancient Romans were great Savory sauce fanciers and used it in a vinegar mixture as a relish for fish and meat dishes in the same way as Mint sauce.

These herbs were known in Britain at an early date, and by the 16th century Savory must have earned in England some fanciful and popular attributes, as Shakespeare referred to it in *The Winter's Tale*, in Perdita's posey of "Hot Lavender, mints, savory, marjoram," of which she said: "These are flowers of middle summer, and, I think, they are given to men of middle age."

"Mercury claims dominion over this herb," wrote Culpepper. "Keep it dry by you all the year, if you love yourself and your ease, and it is a hundred pounds to a penny if you do not." He preferred the Summer Savory to the evergreen one for drying and making into syrups and conserves; he thought it "both hotter and drier than the Winter kind" and not only prescribed it for alleviating bad coughs and "dull spirits in the lethargy, if the juice be snuffed up the nose," but said "dropped into the eyes it clears them of thin humours proceeding from the brain." He also advised that the juice should be heated with oil of Roses and dropped into the ears to remove singing noises and deafness. And for sciatica and palsied limbs, Culpepper would apply a poultice of Savory and wheat flour.

Savory

Most cooks had different uses for this appetizing herb; they put it into stuffings for veal and turkey, into sauces for fish and other things, and it flavoured sausages and pork pies. Still-room workers dried it for pot-pourri and sachets, washing waters and pleasant comforting drinks. It was commonly grown and liked in so many ways that the early emigrants took Savory along with the plants they had relied on at home, to grow in America.

Summer Savory, *S. hortensis*, which means, of the garden, grows about twelve inches high and is a hardy annual to raise from seed sown in spring, when a little patience is required as they germinate very slowly. Its tiny pale lilac flowers bloom in July.

Winter Savory has the advantage of being available all the year round. This dwarf hardy perennial, with woody branching stems, bears its little pale purple blossoms in early summer; it has the characteristically strong, Savory flavour and scent and is used for the same culinary purposes as the annual sort. It is *S. montana*, of the mountains, and accustomed to dry stony ground, and when it is pampered with the luxury of a soil that is very rich it becomes sappy and susceptible to frost. In suitable light or medium soil, this Savory grows into a good-looking bush and will serve the kitchen for several years, but as it grows old it becomes less leafy, so it is advisable to rear new plants every two or three years, either from cuttings in late spring, root division in autumn, or by pegging down a side shoot or two in early summer into the soil, where they will form roots and can be detached from the parent plant.

Parkinson, writing of this Savory, said people used it dried and powdered and mixed with fine breadcrumbs "to breade their meate, be it fish or flesh, to give it a quicker relish." It was considered the best herb for dressing trout.

Like most of the Labiatae family, to which the Savorys belong, they have certain medicinal virtues and are good for relieving flatulence. Winter Savory was one of Culpepper's remedies for colic.

SORREL

Writing in 1720, the great diarist and salad-lover, John Evelyn, said that Sorrel imparted "so grateful a quickness to the salad that it should never be left out." These delicious herbs, of which two kinds are cultivated, owe their pleasant acidity to a special salt, binoxalate of potash, in their make-up. Because of this they are refreshing additions to salads and, in France and other continental countries, to soups, stews, ragouts and fricassees. The two types grown for eating are the French Sorrel or Buckler-leaved Sorrel and the old English Garden Sorrel, Green Sauce, Sour Sauce, Sour Sabs, to quote a few of its ancient names. This grows wild in Britain and in most parts of Europe, and it was commonly grown and used in these islands until the introduction in 1596, of the superior French sort, with its better flavour and fleshier leaves. This much employed continental type is a wilding in mountainous districts of Switzerland, Italy, Southern France, Germany and North Africa. Although it is occasionally found growing wild in Scotland and the north of England, in those places the plants are most probably descended from original garden escapers.

Sorrel is among the oldest of pot-herbs and it had no small reputation as a medicinal one. To quote Evelyn again: "Sorrel sharpens the appetite, assuages heat, cools the liver and strengthens the heart; is an anti-scorbutic, resisting putrefaction and in the making of sallets imparts a grateful quickness to the rest as supplying the want of oranges and lemons. Together with salt, it gives both the name and the relish to sallets from the sapidity, which renders not plants and herbs only, but men themselves pleasant and agreeable."

Culpepper also saw Sorrel as a valuable cooling remedy for fevers and inflammations, and as a refresher of "overspent spirits with the violence of furious or fiery fits of agues." His list of ailments which could be helped by Sorrel was long and impressive and embraced abscesses, boils and the awful plague-sores. He also said: "The distilled water of the herb is of much good use for all the purposes aforesaid." Sorrel water was also a popular drink to improve complexions, the instructions for its making were given in a surviving Tudor household book.

Boerhaave extolled Sorrel for some very useful cures; he said: "No plant better cleanses the body of feculent humours, if the plant be eaten green or its juice drunk; it helps an offensive breath, fastens loose teeth, cures putrefaction of the gums, and is extremely beneficial in all cases where the blood is too fluid and the vessels lax." Gerard described eight different kinds of Sorrel and his belief in the herb's medicinal and culinary virtues tallied with that of most physicians and cooks.

Sorrel's many culinary uses included the ancient and ever popular Sour sauce or Green sauce, served like apple sauce with pork, duck, goose, fish, etc. It was made by beating the herb to pulp and mixing it

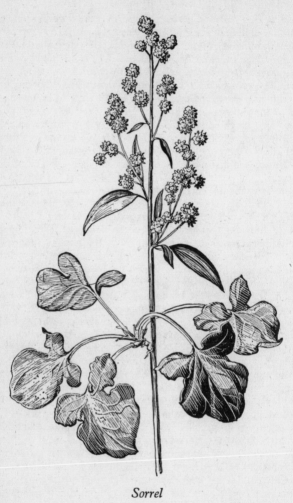

Sorrel

with a little sugar and vinegar. The acid taste of the leaves was also much liked when cooked with only the moisture from the washed leaves, and served as a dressing with rich meats such as veal, lamb, etc. Cooks wrapped and tied Sorrel leaves around tough meat when cooking, to make it more tender.

Pliny said Sorrel rendered meat more pleasant and lighter of digestion, and the Romans used it a great deal as a salad herb, a vegetable for flavouring meat dishes, and they chewed the leaves to prevent thirst. Its generic name *Rumex* is perhaps from the Latin word for a spear in allusion to the shape of its leaves. French Sorrel was called *R. scutatus*, from its shield-shaped leaves; the Garden Sorrel was *R. acetosa*, which meant acid.

The versatile Sorrel may be used like rennet to curdle milk; and the leaves remove certain stains from linen.

French Sorrel is the best kind to grow, making a low-growing lush plant with thickish, very glaucous leaves. It is a hardy perennial and likes a dryish soil and an open situation. The flowering stems should be cut when they form to encourage new tender leaves. Seeds may be sown in spring or, to save time in growing, small plants can be bought from a nursery. To be sure of the most succulent leaves from new plants, make a hole for each one with a trowel and fill it with compost, then set the plants in this and water them well.

SWEET CICELY

Sweet Cicely, Smooth Cicely, Sweet Bracken, Cow Chervil or Sweet Fern—the last name best describes this lovely herb. It is found growing wild on verges and hedge banks in the northern counties of England and Ireland, and along the mountain roads in Scotland, but is not common in the south or in Wales, though Mr. Geoffrey Grigson, in his *The Englishman's Flora* says: "In South Wales I have often noticed Sweet Cicely growing in graveyards, set, I think, as a plant of memory and sweetness around the headstones."

There is some doubt whether Sweet Cicely is really a British native. It may be, but in Lancashire it is known as the Roman Plant, which might be a clue to its original introduction. In any case it is now at home here and has gained not only a number of local names, most of them alluding to its sweetness, but also an ancient reputation as a pot-herb once grown in every garden. Turner, in the 16th century, wrote: "I

Sweet Cicely

never saw greater plenty of it than I have seen in the hortyard of Pembroke Hall in Cambridge, where I was sometime a poore fellow."

When describing this herb, most writers have likened it to Hemlock. Parkinson wrote of its "divers faire and great winged leaves" and said it was "in show very like unto Hemlockes, of a good and pleasant smell and taste which have caused us to term it Sweet Chervil." Culpepper also said: "It groweth like the Hemlock, but of a fresher green colour, tasting as sweet as the Aniseed." The leaves are like lace ferns and are often flecked with white, and their undersides are slightly downy. They taste like a mixture of a little Anise and a bit of Lovage sprinkled with castor sugar. Most people writing of it remark on this sugared effect.

Sweet Cicely, *Myrrhis odorata* (both names mean fragrant), is one of the most attractive members of the Umbelliferae group, bearing its umbrellas of bee-haunted white flowers in early summer on stems eventually reaching five feet tall, but it is a slow grower and takes a few years to achieve its greatness. The fruits, the "seeds," are an inch long and very flavorous. The name Cicely arose from *seseli* or *seselis*, from Greek through Latin, by assimilation to the women's name. The plant's natural home is in the mountain pastures of the Pyrenees to the Caucasus but it now flourishes over much of Europe.

All parts of Sweet Cicely have been used for culinary purposes. The roots were shredded into salads, and they were boiled; the leaves were put into salads, soups, stews and other dishes; the green seeds were much liked in a salad, and when ripe they were employed as a flavouring spice. This plant is seldom tasted nowadays in English cookery, but it is generally used in Germany and is particularly important in French cooking and is partnered with Tarragon in many dishes. Once it was as popular in England. Gerard said the leaves were "exceeding good, holsome and pleasant among other sallade herbes, giving the taste of Anise seed unto the rest." And he thought "the seeds eaten as a sallad whiles they are yet greene with oile, vinegar and pepper, exceed all other sallads by many degrees, both in pleasantness of taste, sweetness of smell, and wholesomeness for the cold and feeble stomacke." The boiled roots eaten with oil and vinegar was a dish that Gerard considered to be "very good for old people that are dull and without courage; it rejoiceth and comforteth the heart and increaseth their lust and strength." John Evelyn, too, commended Sweet Cicely as "being exceedingly wholesome and chearing the spirits." And all the old herbalists agreed that the herb was "so harmless you cannot use it amiss."

An interesting use for the seeds by people in the north of England was for polishing oak furniture and floors. When the surfaces were dry they were rubbed down with a soft cloth and the result was a high polish and a pleasant scent.

Modern herbalists confirm the old beliefs in the curative value of Sweet Cicely, and it is still prescribed for bladder disorders, flatulence and coughs. It is good for diabetics and an excellent stimulant for "old people," and girls in their teens.

This hardy perennial herb likes a shady, sheltered bed of moisture-holding soil.

TANSY

The handsome Tansy with its crowns of yellow button flowers borne in large heads up to three feet high was grown in herb gardens for so long that it escaped and became naturalized in parts of our country-side. It is now seldom cultivated except in very old gardens, and this neglect is our loss, for its fern-like foliage is as decorative as dark green Prince-of-Wales's feathers, and is pleasantly aromatic. This is one of the herbs which spicily scent a garden on hot summer days.

Tansy is a member of the Daisy family, Compositae. Its botanical names *Tanacetum vulgare*, and its common name Tansy, with the French, *tanaisie*, were all corruptions of *Athanasia*, the Greek word for immortality. Tansy was considered deathless because of the long life of the flowers, Gerard said "because the yellow floures gathered in due time dye not of a long time after." The ancient monk-herbalists so valued the Tansy that they assumed Lucian, the Greek satirist, referred to it when he wrote the passage containing Jupiter's instructions to Mercury to take Ganymede away—"and when he has tasted immortality let him return to us." They then named the herb *Athanasia* and at an early date dedicated it to the Virgin Mary. Another reason for the name was Tansy's virtue in preserving corpses.

Tansy's local names include Bachelor's Buttons, Bitter Buttons, Ginger Plant, Scented Fern, Stinking Elshander, Stinking Willie. (In fairness to many lovely plants it should be remembered that long ago stink was the only word in the language expressive of scent or smell, good or bad.)

For many centuries Tansy was medicinally important for the treatment of several ailments, particularly wounds and disorders of the

Tansy

kidneys and womb. It was used externally by women desiring children, or internally by those who preferred abortion. Hot fomentations of Tansy were applied to sprains and rheumatic pains, and Tansy tea relieved fever and was a cordial.

As a necessity to the well-being of family life Tansy was taken by settlers to New England, where it did very well for itself, becoming happily naturalized in the eastern states of the U.S.

Tansy was particularly popular among the medieval strewing herbs because of its power of discouraging flies and fleas (a high recommendation in the days when floors remained inches thick with debris from many feasts), it was also rubbed on meat in summer to protect it from blow-flies. And it was much fancied as a food-flavouring; the Dutch physician Boerhaave, declared that "this balsamic plant may well supply the place of nutmegs and cinnamon, for I believe that Asia does not supply a plant of greater fragrance than the Tansy."

By the 17th century, the church had claimed Tansy as a holy herb and made it commemorative of the Bitter Herbs of the Passover, to be eaten only at Easter. This ruling annoyed Nicholas Culpepper who wrote in 1652: "Now, forsooth, tansies must be eaten only on Palm and Easter Sundays and their neighbour days," and he gave warning that "want of commonly eating this herb in spring makes people sickly in summer." The earlier habit of eating Tansy and drinking Tansy tea in spring originated in the belief that it counteracted the bad effects of the salted fish and meat which formed a great part of winter's diet.

The old custom of eating Tansy puddings on Easter Sunday still survives in Lincolnshire, where the plant is called "Ginger." The leaves, when used sparingly, have a delicate rather gingerish taste, and they are the flavouring recommended in many 18th-century recipes.

The cultivation of Tansy presents no difficulty as it will grow in any fertile soil. The creeping roots spread quickly making large clumps which may be lifted and divided every three years. Pieces of the root should be planted in April one foot apart. The flower-heads should be removed when they fade.

Tansy is attractive as a foliage plant, its richly coloured, feathery leaves which rather resemble those of Yarrow contrast particularly well with the greyish, simpler foliage of many other herbaceous large-flowered plants, and with such herbs as Sage, Borage, Costmary, etc.

It is best to grow Tansy in a confined space, as when planted in a border it quickly spreads and envelops other subjects. An effective trick to cope with its invasive roots is to plant it invisibly restricted in a bottomless container such as an old bath-tub or pig-trough buried in the soil.

TARRAGON

Tarragon, the Little Dragon, Estragon of the French, probably derives its name, through the Arabic, from the Greek *drakon*, a serpent; its specific name, *dracunculus*, means a little dragon. It was so called because in olden times they supposed it had the power of curing any bites or stings from venomous creatures, including serpents and mad dogs.

This herb has no long history of curing man's maladies; the fresh leaves contain an essential volatile oil identical with that of Anise, and are good to relieve flatulence and digestive upsets, but the oil is completely lost in the dried herb. The plant was once considered to be an aphrodisiac and its roots a cure for toothache. Writing of Tarragon, John Evelyn said: "'Tis highly cordial and friend to the head, heart and liver," and Gerard related an old theory of Tarragon's growing from the seed of flax put into a radish root, or sea onion, and set in the ground, which will bring forth this herb.

Tarragon's greatest services have been its culinary successes, particularly in continental cookery, its warm flavour being appreciated as a contrast to that of cooler-tasting herbs, and it is one of the most important of flavourings in many countries.

There are two species of Tarragon, the French Tarragon, which is a native of South Europe and parts of Asia, and the Russian Tarragon, a Siberian wild plant. The French sort is the smaller plant, about two and a half feet tall, with shiny leaves of a medium green colour and a strongly aromatic taste. This one is properly called *Artemisia dracunculus*. The Russian kind is *A. dracunculoides*, meaning resembling *dracunculus*, and compared with the French type it is valueless as a flavouring herb. It grows from three to five feet high and its pale-green leaves resemble those of Willow. They are eaten in Persia as an appetizer.

These Artemisias are closely related to Lad's Love, Southernwood, and are of the Compositae family, but the Little Dragon's tiny greenish Daisy flowers scarcely open away from its homeland.

French Tarragon is not one of the easiest of culinary herbs to grow, but it repays the little extra effort to accommodate it with the pleasure of being able to cut leaves from sturdy, good-looking plants. As in the

Tarragon

case of all herbs, the taste of Tarragon when freshly gathered is in every way superior to the flavour of either wilting foliage from the market or the dried leaves from a packet. To grow lush and achieve its most delicious, rich flavour, Tarragon requires as warm and sunny a position as possible, and to have reasonable protection from cutting winds from the north and easterly directions. Its ideal soil is lightish but rich in humus, and it must be well drained. The fleshy roots are brittle and they easily rot if their bed is at all water-logged in winter. This risk should not arise if the bed is raised a little as suggested for a herb garden. The plant is a hardy perennial, and when happily placed and generously supplied with good compost it should be successful. Actually, a lot of Tarragon plants survived the severe winter of 1962-3, in districts where a number of herbs considered to be more hardy succumbed.

Tarragon is not generally raised from seed in France or England as it seldom produces fertile flowers, and it is advisable to buy the first plants from a reputable herb nursery that will be certain to supply the right type, the true French Tarragon, *A. dracunculus*. Unfortunately a great many Russian Tarragon plants are mistakenly sold as the desirable French kind.

Planting should be done in April, setting the roots two or three inches deep and about a foot apart. The second season when the plants are established, new ones should be started in May, from pieces of root with a shoot showing; these should be carefully severed from the plant with a sharp knife. This re-stocking is necessary as the old plants deteriorate after a few seasons.

Tarragon may be enjoyed in winter if, in September, a few roots are set in a box of soil, or in pots, and kept in a warm greenhouse. Or, failing the greenhouse, it would be worth trying the pots on a sunny window-sill in a warm room.

The foliage sprays may be cut and dried in late summer; and in autumn the bed should be protected from frost with a top-dressing of compost and a little straw which will provide for them a banquet in spring.

THYME

The scent of Thyme means much more than the appetizing savour of stuffing for roasted poultry. It was one of the special odours of ancient cities in their heyday.

To the Greeks this herb signified not only courage, but style, grace and elegance for whom "to smell of Thyme" was a term of high praise. It was the most fashionable masculine scent with which Athenian, and then Roman, gentlemen perfumed their chests after bathing. The smoke of Thyme burning as incense and as a fumigant drifted from temples and public buildings in classical towns. Virgil alluded to it as an effective fumigant, and Pliny said that when burnt it put to flight venomous creatures. Its antiseptic qualities were well understood by the ancients.

Thyme gave a brave flavour to many dishes; and it was grown over vast areas to feed Greek and Roman bees and give a particular flavour to their honey, the best of which came from Mount Hymettus near Athens and was famous for its delicious taste and sweetness.

The Romans were especially fond of Thyme in cheeses, and they flavoured a liqueur with it. They brought the herb with its high reputation to Britain, where its use persisted long after they had left and the fancy for bathing had lapsed. Medieval ladies embroidered sprays of Thyme, with a bee, on scarves for their knights, as the emblem of courage.

Thyme vinegar was for centuries used to relieve headaches, and many other ailments were treated with the herb, Thyme's medicinal qualities were genuine, being based on its essential oil, Thymol, which is still much used. The pounded herb mixed with syrup relieved whooping-cough and sore throat; Thyme tea comforted wind and colic; Thyme ointment was applied to gout and rheumatic swellings, and in the 16th century, Gerard claimed Thyme would cure sciatica, leprosy and the falling sickness. Some years later, Culpepper said it was a noble strengthener of the lungs and took away any pains and hardness of the spleen. And he maintained with truth that "it is so harmless you need not fear the use of it."

Curiously, Thyme has no local names beyond those which qualify it, such as "Mother Thyme," etc. It is a bushy perennial of the Labiatae family, and a native of the Mediterranean regions. Garden Thyme is a cultivated form of Wild Thyme, *Thymus serpyllum*, the many varieties of which are among the most useful herbs for culinary purposes and for furnishing a garden. They are all evergreen, varying in flavour, and the colour of their foliage and their blossoms vary through all shades of rose-pink, mauve, crimson and purple to white. The types most often used for flavouring food, Common Thyme or Black Thyme, and the

Thyme

Lemon Thymes, make cushion-like plants, others provide creeping herbs for crevices between bricks or stones or they carpet paved walks. They were one of Francis Bacon's garden pleasures, and in his plan for the perfect garden, he directed the planting of paths with Thyme and other herbs which when trodden perfume the air "most delightfully." All Thymes are edible and the scented ones are good for flavouring or making pot-pourris.

Thymes are easily grown in a sunny position in dryish, open, gritty soil. They lack flavour when planted in heavy wet ground, and such soil should be broken up with plenty of coarse sand or grit and limestone chippings mixed into the bed. Thyme has a better flavour when grown from rooted-cuttings than when raised from seed.

Some of the most desirable Thymes for use and decoration are *Thymus vulgaris*, the Common or Black Thyme; *T. citriodorus*, Lemon-scented and its varieties "Silver Queen" with silvery foliage, and *T. c. aureus*, with golden leaves, which makes a good pot-plant. *T. fragrantissimus*, deliciously orange-scented, is also enjoyable as a pot-plant. *T. azoricas*, the pine-scented type, makes a flat cushion of green leaves and pale purple flowers. *T. Herba-Barona*, the Caraway-scented Thyme of rather prostrate growth, is a good pot-plant. *T. mastachinus*, R. Armstrong's variety, lavender-scented with greyish hairy leaves, is a trailing kind for paving. Two good varieties of the carpeting Wild Thyme, *Thymus serpyllum*, are the white-flowered *T. s. albus*, and *T. s.* variety *lanuginosus floribundus*, with grey woolly leaves and rich purple blossoms.

VIOLET

The Sweet Scented Violet, *Viola odorata*, the ancient flower of love, was chosen by the Greeks for its perfume as Aphrodite's flower, which she shared with her son Priapus, the god of all fertility. The Greeks called it *ione*, because when Jupiter, fearing the violent jealousy of Juno, changed his beloved Io into a white heifer, he created Violets for her to eat.

The Greeks and Romans loved Violets and used them in every possible way. Athenians suffering insomnia drank sleeping draughts made from them; some took Violets to comfort and strengthen their hearts; they allayed immoderate anger with them; and delayed intoxication when feasting by wearing crowns of Violets. So did the Romans, and they drank a great deal of Violet wine; and put the leaves in salads and made Violet conserves, Violet perfume and cosmetics.

For gouty Romans, Pliny prescribed a liniment of Violet roots and vinegar, which he also commended for troublesome spleens. Violet garlands or chaplets, he said, worn around the head, not only dispelled the fumes of wine but would relieve headaches and dizziness. Tons of Violets were raised at Paestum to provide some of the vast quantities needed by the rich Mediterranean communities.

The ancient Britons too used Violet cosmetics and believed the flowers steeped in goat's milk made their women's faces fair. The Anglo-Saxons esteemed this herb for curing new wounds and stubborn old sores. And Violets were still advised for insomnia in Askham's 10th-century *Herbal*: "For them that may not slepe for sickness seeth this herb in water and at even let him soke well hys feete in the water to the ancles, wha he goeth to bed, bind of this herbe to his temples."

The love for Violets and the belief in their many virtues never lessened; they were grown by monks in their physic yards, and pre-scribed by them for many ills. When private gardens were made, Violets were among the first flowers to be cultivated for pleasure and for use in the still-room, where for many centuries they made medicines, syrups, perfumes, conserves, cosmetics, with many sweetly-scented things; small pillows were stuffed with them; wine was made from them; the leaves and the flowers were candied as sweetmeats and decorations for sweet puddings. Some puddings were made from them. An ancient French recipe for "Vyolette," instructed the cook to boil Violet flowers beat them to pulp, then mix them with milk, rice flour and sugar or honey, and colour the result with Violets.

"Violet Plate" was a favourite conserve during Charles II's reign, and was sold by all apothecaries as a mild laxative.

Culpepper said of the Violet: "It is a fine pleasing plant of Venus, of a mild nature and no way hurtful." He described its many medical uses and recommended poultices of the leaves for reducing inflamed swell-ings. Modern herbalists have claimed some astonishing cures from such poultices applied along with infusions taken.

The generic name *Viola* is the ancient Latin name for the Violet, which is of the *Violaceae* order.

To provide the best flowers in good quantity, Violet beds must be re-planted annually with sturdy plants from last season's runners. The bed should be in an open westerly position not too shaded nor in full

Violet

sun during summer. Dig the soil deeply a few weeks before planting, and mix in some coarse sand if necessary, some well-decayed manure or compost, leaf-mould and bonfire ash. A quilt of leaf-mould placed on the surface after planting keeps the soil moist and cool and rich. The day before lifting the new plants it is advisable to water them thoroughly to prevent their wilting when moved. Set them nine inches apart both ways, and puddle them in. Keep them moist until settled. They need plenty of water in summer and a fortnightly treat of liquid manure before and during flowering.

The plants may be put into a cold frame in autumn for winter-flowering, one that has been made for melons or cucumbers suits them.

Violets are very susceptible to Red Spider; this cannot be seen but must be suspected when foliage turns yellow. If this happens, the plants must be sprayed all over as directed, with a preparation sold for the purpose of eradicating this pest.

II. Flavours—Herbs in the Kitchen

THE most useful utensils for coping with culinary herbs, for mincing, pounding, cutting and chopping, straining jellies, etc., are:

a Mouli "Parsmint" herb mincer
a mortar and pestle
sharp scissors
a wooden chopping board
a nylon "hair-sieve"
a garlic juice presser.

The term *Fines Herbes* often used in continental recipes applies in general to:

Chervil, Chives, Parsley and Tarragon.

The traditional *Bouquet Garni* consists of a Bay leaf, sprigs of Thyme and Parsley, tied together with thread so that the bundle may be suspended in the stew, soup, etc., while cooking, and can be easily removed before dishing-up. But a garnishing bouquet should be varied to suit the ingredients of the dish it is to flavour, according to the herbs which blend most happily with them. To help with this choice, the most suitable herbs are listed in this book with the different foods they complement.

Cooks with only small gardens or a few pots of herbs, grown for flavouring, can order from the greengrocer the greater quantities needed for certain recipes, as most of the roots and leaves, such as Chervil, Fennel and Dill, are available for foreign restaurateurs in all the large vegetable markets.

APPETIZERS

Mint and Rue are both herbs that whet the appetite, and though Mint may be used generously and in many ways, the rather bitter-tasting Rue should be eaten sparingly.

RUE SANDWICHES

Are excellent with a glass of apéritif and particularly with Vermouth, but just two leaves per sandwich are enough. They should be chopped fine and mixed with the butter to spread between small, very thin, slices of bread.

CANAPÉS

To make these, cut some small bread rolls into equal halves, scoop out all the crumb and place the crusts to dry in a cool oven. For filling, chop fine some hard-boiled eggs (about 1 egg to 4 crust-cases according to size), chop finely some Tarragon, Chervil and Chives. Put them together in a basin, season with salt and pepper to taste, and mix with a little olive oil and a few drops of Tarragon vinegar, then fill the crust-cases. Fillets of anchovies or sardines may be placed on top.

Canapés can be varied after experimenting with different herb flavours. When topped with sardines, lobster, crab, shrimps, prawns or cold fish, Fennel is another good choice of herb.

HERB CHEESE CANAPÉS

For these, you cut some very thin slices of bread and stamp them out into shapes with a pastry-cutter, then fry them to a light brown in a little butter. Smear mustard on these croûtons and place some herb-cheese on top. Toast them quickly under the grill and serve hot.

The herb-cheese mixture for savoury canapés may be made from one of the herb-cheese recipes, or it can consist of almost any sort of mild-flavoured cheese like cheshire, cheddar, processed, etc., grated and mixed with some such herbs as Mint, Parsley, Chives, Thymes, Sage, Lovage, Marjoram, Basil, etc.

BISCUITS

HERB BISCUITS

Of various flavours are produced by adding either a blended variety of herbs or a single herb to any kind of pastry or to a plain biscuit mixture. For this, you mix to a soft dough 1 lb. of self-raising flour, a pinch of salt, 1 egg, well beaten, ½-cupful of milk. Turn out on to a floured pastry-board and divide into 3 or 4 separate pieces, to each of which may be added chopped herbs of different flavours. Knead the dough with the chosen herbs and roll out thinly. Cut into circles, prick the tops and lay the biscuits on a greased baking-sheet. Bake 5 to 10 minutes in a hot oven.

MINT PUFF BISCUITS

Are generally liked and are made with puff, rough-puff or flaky pastry mixed with finely-chopped Mint and rolled thin. Then they are cut into shapes, placed on a greased baking-sheet and baked quickly in a hot oven.

ROSEMARY AND TANSY

Should be tried together for their delicate gingerish flavour, in a pastry or biscuit mixture.

CHEESE STRAWS

Are delicious with herbs added. They may be made with any kind of pastry rolled out and thickly spread with grated cheese and chopped herbs, then folded, rolled again, and once more spread, folded and rolled, then cut into strips for "straws." The strips should be spread apart on a baking-sheet and baked quickly until a light golden colour.

CHEESE BISCUITS

With herbs. To make these, rub 3 oz. of butter into 8 oz. of flour with a pinch of salt and a pinch of cayenne pepper. Add 8 oz. of grated cheese and about 3 tablespoonfuls of chopped herbs. Beat up an egg with a little cold water and stir it in to make a stiff dough, then turn this out on to a floured pastry-board, knead in the herbs, roll thin, cut into shapes and prick the tops. Place the biscuits on a greased baking-sheet and bake 10 to 15 minutes till pale golden brown.

Sage and Chives, Mint and Marjoram, and Thymes of different flavours are especially good with cheese in biscuits.

BREAD

WITH HERBS

Bread is given unusual piquancy by flavouring with certain herbs. Some Roman bakers placed bundles of Fennel under loaves in the oven to give them a distinctive taste. Bread baked on sprigs of Rosemary used to be considered a cure for a lost sense of smell or for giddiness.

Caraway or Dill seeds inside and on top of loaves are understandably popular in many countries. And Poppy seeds sprinkled on bread, rolls or cakes, before cooking, give a deliciously nutty flavour to the crust.

PULLED BREAD

As made centuries ago, is particularly good to eat with herb butters or herb cheese. For this you pull out the crumb of a fresh loaf and divide it into rocky-looking pieces, place these on a baking-sheet lined with paper and bake them to a light golden colour. They must be quite crisp.

BUTTERS

HERB BUTTERS

May be homely mixtures or famous ones. The simple sorts have many uses. For instance, they make delicious backgrounds for savoury sandwiches, they may be spread on biscuits, on fish or baked potatoes and other vegetables, and they are good served with cheese. Their flavouring may consist of a blend of several herbs or it can be limited to a single flavour such as Chives, any of the Mints, Parsley, Sage, Tarragon, etc. These homely butters are easily made by adding to a ½-teacupful of creamed butter 2 tablespoonfuls of finely-chopped or minced herbs and a teaspoonful of lemon juice.

CHIVRY BUTTER

Contains a blend of Parsley, Tarragon, Shallot, Chives and Burnet.

MAÎTRE D'HÔTEL BUTTER

Is the favourite garnish to spread over any broiled or grilled meat, especially steak or fish when ready for table; then it is set in the oven for a few minutes so that the butter may penetrate the meat. To create this you mix 3 sprigs of Parsley, chopped very fine, with 2 oz. of butter, the juice of half a lemon, salt and pepper to taste, and Chives may be added with advantage.

GREEN BUTTER

Much used in the last century, this contains a rich blend of herbs and can be made simply as ordinary herb butters, but here is the old "chef's" recipe. Cream 2 oz. of butter. Pound to pulp in a mortar ½ a clove of Garlic, 2 small Shallots, a good spray of Chervil, 2 sprigs of Water Cress, 6 sprays of Parsley, a small teaspoonful of salt and a good pinch of cayenne pepper. Then add the butter and pound together. Rub through a sieve and keep cool till wanted. A few drops of green colouring should be added if the butter lacks its proper tint.

MONTPELIER BUTTER

To ¼ lb. of butter allow 1 shallot, 1 clove of Garlic, the yolks of 2 hard-boiled eggs, a dessertspoonful of Tarragon vinegar, 3 anchovies or sardines, 1 oz. each of Parsley, Chervil, Water Cress and Chives. Rub the Garlic around the bowl before adding the ingredients. Chop the herbs finely and remove tails, skin and bone from the fish. Then pound together in the Garlic-scented bowl, add the vinegar last and season with salt and cayenne pepper to taste. Rub through a sieve and shape into balls ready for use.

RAVIGOTE BUTTER

Needs equal quantities of Chives, Chervil, Burnet, Tarragon, Cress, a few Capers or Nasturtium seeds and a clove of Garlic. Weigh the herbs and allow twice their weight of butter. Pound them together with a little olive oil to blend, add a few drops of juice from shallots and season with salt and cayenne pepper.

GREEN DYE

Is made by pounding sufficient Spinach or Parsley in a mortar and squeezing the juice through muslin, then warming it so that it blends with the butter, but it must not boil.

All herb butters should be of a nice green tint and if more colour is needed it should be applied either by making this dye or with a few drops of a good vegetable dye bought from a reputable herb shop.

ROSE-PETAL BUTTER

Makes a special party delicacy. It is made by placing the required amount of fresh butter, wrapped in paper, in a pot that is large enough to contain sufficient strongly scented Rose petals to completely surround the package. The jar must be covered closely and left for 24 hours so that the Rose fragrance penetrates the butter.

The Rose-petal sandwiches spread with this butter should be cut into shapes and contain a Rose petal or two slightly protruding, and petals should be scattered around the edge of the plate.

HERB BUTTER FOR BEEF STEAKS

Is especially good when blended with Chervil, Sweet Cicely and Tarragon. This mixture should also be tried on fish steaks.

WATER CRESS BUTTER

Is pleasant for sandwiches (especially of cold chicken, tomato or ham), for steaks, on potatoes, broad beans, and other vegetables.

To make it, wash and dry the Water Cress, chop it finely or mince it, and to every 1½ tablespoonfuls of the minced herb allow 2 oz. of butter.

CAKES

CARAWAY SEED CAKE

Is probably the most familiar example of the use of herb-flavouring in cakes. The seeds are added to a good plain cake mixture and are sprinkled on top of the cake before baking. Anise and Dill seeds are used in the same way and have a similar flavour.

POPPY CAKES

Are popular in many countries, made with the seeds inside the mixture and sprinkled on top of the cake before cooking.

Poppy seeds are delicious and should be tried generously sprinkled on the tops of fruit cakes, plain cakes, orange or lemon sponges, before they are put into the oven; they have a nutty flavour when cooked.

GOOSNARGH CAKES

Rely also on aromatic seeds. To make them, rub 6 oz. of butter into 8 oz. of flour with 1 oz. of castor sugar and a sprinkling of Caraway seeds and Coriander seeds. No moisture. Roll out about ¼ of an inch thick and cut into circles. Sift a thick layer of castor sugar on top and leave the cakes for 24 hours before baking in a moderate oven. When cooked, shake more sugar over them.

LEMON OR ORANGE CAKE WITH CORIANDER SEEDS

Make a creamed mixture with 5 oz. of butter, 5 oz. of castor sugar, 2 well-beaten eggs, the grated rind and juice of a lemon or orange, a little milk if necessary, and a teaspoonful of Coriander seeds. Mix in 8 oz. of self-raising flour, then put into a greased baking-tin and sprinkle a few Coriander seeds on top. Bake in a moderate oven for about an hour.

FLANNEL CAKES

Were a very old bun recipe which included fresh elder blossoms beaten into the batter to give a light fluffy texture and delicate flavour.

To make them, melt a piece of butter the size of a walnut in 1 pint of milk, when lukewarm add the yolk and white of an egg—beaten separately—then stir it into 6 oz. of plain flour. Add 1 oz. of yeast and the fresh blossoms stripped from 2 large flower-heads, beat the mixture well, and leave it to rise in a warm place for about 45 minutes, or until it has doubled its size. Then put it into large greased bun or muffin tins, allowing room for further rising. Bake for 15 minutes in a hot oven.

CHEESE

Most herb flavours are good for cheese dishes, but the best results are usually gained from Basil, Caraway, Chives, Parsley, Sage, Marjorams and the Thymes. Any of these herbs may be used in soufflés, Welsh Rarebits or any cheese concoction.

CHEESE OF SEVEN HERBS

An ancient Cumberland recipe, has 2 tablespoonfuls of finely-chopped mixed herbs—Chives, Chervil, Parsley, Sage, Tarragon, Thyme, Winter Savory, mixed with 4 oz. of grated cheese, 2 tablespoonfuls of cream and 3 tablespoonfuls of sherry. The ingredients are gently stirred in a double saucepan until melted and creamy. Then the mixture is put into small pots for use when cold.

MILK CHEESE

Can be made savoury and varied to suit all tastes by the addition of herbs. In fact, the number of appetite-provoking flavours this home-made cheese can assume is limited only by the cook's imagination and supply of herbs.

The basis of this sort of cheese is made with the solid curds of milk "turned" either during hot weather or by rennet. These are strained through a bag of muslin that is fine enough in texture to hold the curd but allow the whey to drain off when it is suspended over a bowl. The bag must be kept clear of the escaping sour liquid. The drained curds are placed in a basin and mashed with salt and pepper to taste, and the finely chopped or minced herbs. A few drops of Garlic juice are especially good with Sage, Mint, Marjoram or the Thymes, and Chives' delicate onion-like flavour is tasty with most herbs.

SAVOURY FLANS OR SAVOURY CHEESE CAKES

May be made from this milk cheese by adding butter and eggs. In to $\frac{1}{4}$ lb. of the curds mix 2 oz. of butter, a beaten egg and the minced herbs. Line a flan tin or patty tins with flaky pastry and add the cheese and herb filling. Bake quickly in a hot oven until just set.

MILK CHEESE "CREAM"

To be eaten with jam or fruit, is made from curds without salt and pepper, but delicately flavoured with 2 or 3 tender young Lavender leaves, minced, or Rosemary and Tansy together for a subtle suggestion of ginger or Balm for a lemony tang.

CONSERVES

Now almost forgotten pleasures, were ancient Greek and Roman delicacies and remained deservedly popular until nearly a century ago, being eaten when fancied, as a relish for meat or game, as sweetmeats, or as medicines. They were made by beating up the freshly gathered green tops or flowers with 3 times their weight of sugar. Any suitable herbs or flowers were used, but the flavours generally liked were Lavender, Mint, Rose, Rosemary and Violet.

LAVENDER CONSERVE

Seldom absent from Queen Elizabeth I's table, was a relish for any meat dish or fruit salad, and a favourite sweetmeat. It was also eaten to relieve headaches.

MINT CONSERVE

Added its famous zest to any cold meat dish and green or fruit salad, and provided a delicious remedy for flatulence.

ROSE CONSERVE

Was most fancied as a sweetmeat, or was used with puddings or thinly spread on dainty sandwiches. It was considered highly effective for relieving faintness or bouts of coughing.

ROSEMARY CONSERVE

One of the most popular kinds, gave its aromatic savour to any dish, and its easing comfort for headaches, coughs or indigestion.

VIOLET CONSERVE

Known as "Violet Plate" in the reign of Charles II, was usually placed on dining-tables to provide a relish for any dish or to be eaten as a sweetmeat. And it had the reputation of being a kindly, gentle laxative and a soother of coughs.

DESSERT

The use of Caraway seeds as a garnish for dessert with either raw or cooked fruit is a pleasant old-fashioned custom that was probably already common in ancient Greece and Rome, and the taste persisted for centuries. Shakespeare refers to the habit in his *Henry IV*, where Squire Shallow invites Falstaff to "a pippin and a dish of caraways." Roast apples are still served accompanied by a small saucer of Caraway seeds, not only at Trinity College, Cambridge, but also at the Dinner of some of the old London Livery Companies.

DRINKS

ANGELICA LIQUEUR

Is delicious and digestive. To make it, you put 1 oz. of freshly gathered Angelica stem, chopped up and steeped in 1 pint of brandy, with 1 oz. of skinned bitter Almonds pulped in a mortar. Leave for

5 days then strain through fine muslin and add 1 pint of cold syrup. To make the syrup, dissolve ¾ lb. of white sugar with ½ pint of water; bring it gently to the boil, stirring until the sugar is dissolved, then let it cool before adding to the liqueur.

ELDER-BERRY SYRUP

Is an excellent remedy for colds, and a favourite old winter "night-cap." Allow a wine-glassful in a tumbler with hot water, and sugar if liked.

To make it, pick the ripe berries from the stalks and stew with a little water in a jar in the oven or pan. After straining allow ¼ oz. of whole ginger and 9 cloves to 4 pints of juice. Boil the ingredients an hour, strain again and bottle.

CUPS AND PUNCHES

Should be decorated with sprays of cordial herbs. Borage, Balm, Burnet or Verbena are used for such cups as Claret, Chablis, Cider, Mixed Fruit, Rhubarb and Raspberry, and also for Milk Punch. Mint is the herb for Ale or Pineapple Cups.

WINES

Made with herbs can be very good, especially from Balm, Elder-flowers, Elderberries, Parsley, Rose-hips and Rose petals, and making wine at home is not difficult when the principles are sufficiently explained and understood; but as there are numerous books devoted entirely to its pleasurable possibilities wine-making is considered to be beyond the scope of this work.

EGG DISHES

The choice of herbs to use with egg dishes depends on the manner of cooking. When BAKED, use any of the following types, either singly or in mixtures, Chervil, Chives, Parsley, Tarragon, Thymes, Costmary, Basil. For OMELETTES, Chives, Parsley, Tarragon, and Thymes are liked. Sage and Chives together are good with a filling of chopped ham or bacon. And Parsley, Mint, Marjoram and Tarragon suit a mushroom filling. Some of the herbs should be cooked with the omelette and the rest sprinkled over it before serving.

SCRAMBLED EGGS

May be flavoured with any of the omelette herbs. A tasty "scramble" can be mixed by cooking some peeled and chopped tomatoes in butter, then adding the eggs, some chopped Parsley, Basil, Tarragon and a small pinch of Lemon Thyme, and stirring together until just setting.

This mixture is excellent cold as a sandwich filling.

BAKED CUSTARD

Should be tried with one of its old-time flavourings, either the subtle almond-like one from a leaf of common Laurel, or the aromatic taste of a Bay leaf.

EGG CUSTARD SAUCE

Is delicious as it used to be served before the introduction of custard powder. To make it bring to the boil 1 pint of milk with a Bay leaf, or a Laurel leaf, in it. Add 3 oz. of castor sugar and let it cool slightly. Beat up 2 eggs, pour the milk on the eggs and mix. Remove the leaf and put the mixture into a double-saucepan of boiling water. Stir until the custard thickens, it must not boil. A teaspoonful of brandy may be added before serving.

SAVOURY PANCAKES

Can be flavoured with the same herbs as omelettes and given a variety of fillings.

ROYALES

A savoury custard served in France with soups is made with 1 whole egg and 3 egg yolks whisked and added to 1 gill of boiling consommé. The mixture is put into a well-buttered gallipot and placed in a pan containing about 3 inches of hot water, then cooked in a gentle oven for about 15 minutes, until set. When cold the solid custard is turned out and cut into shapes. The French give a great variety of flavours to royales, and two of the most popular herb ones are ROYALE AU CHER-FEUIL (Chervil), and ROYALE À L'ESTRAGON (Tarragon); these are made by putting the chosen herb into the consommé to flavour it before adding it to the eggs. Other herbs can be effectively used in the same manner.

SEASONED PUDDING

Is an appetizing and useful herb-flavoured elaboration of the true Yorkshire Pudding, for which an authentic receipt is: Add a well-beaten egg to ¼ lb. of flour and stir in gradually ½ pint of milk. Season with ¼ teaspoonful of salt and a dash of pepper, and let the smooth, creamy batter stand for at least ½ hour. To cook, heat a little dripping in a roasting tin and when sizzling hot pour in the batter and add plenty of chopped cooked onion, sultanas, minced Sage and Marjoram, or any other mixture of herbs as fancied, and bake about 20 minutes in a hot oven. Serve cut in squares with rich gravy.

POACHED EGG ON WATER CRESS PURÉE

Makes an attractive supper or luncheon dish. Make the purée by boiling the Water Cress in very little water, then rub it through a sieve and mix it with a little cream and a pinch of salt. Lay it on croûtons of fried bread with a poached egg on top.

FISH

Herbs flavour a number of delicious sauces designed to accompany fish dishes, and they are also used in the cooking of fish.

WHITEFISH STEAKS

May be cooked in a casserole with a garnish of chopped Chives, a spray of Parsley, of Fennel or Dill, and a thin slice of butter. When cooked, a sauce should be made with the liquor to which more of the fresh herbs may be added.

A SIMPLE STUFFING

Of breadcrumbs, bound with a little butter and a beaten egg, and containing minced Tarragon, Parsley, Chervil and Lemon Thyme, will change the most common-place fish cut into a desirable dish.

FISH FILLETS OR STEAKS

Are good dipped into herb-seasoned batter and fried.

CURRIED FISH

Is enriched with Coriander seeds.

THE MOST SUITABLE HERBS TO ACCOMPANY FISH

For *Crab*, Sage, Tarragon, Thyme. *Lobster*, Chervil, Thyme, Tarragon. *Mussels* and *Scallops*, Chervil, Tarragon, Thyme, Sorrel. *Salmon* and *Mackerel*, Fennel, Dill, Marjoram, Tarragon. *Shrimps*, Basil, Bay, Dill, Tarragon. *Sole*, Bay, Marjoram, Tarragon, Parsley. Any *White Fish*, Bay, Basil, Chives, Dill, Fennel, Parsley, Marjoram, Tarragon. *Herrings*, Bay, Parsley, Thyme, Capers or Nasturtium seeds, fresh or pickled.

Winter Savory, chopped fine or minced, and mixed with grated breadcrumbs, used to be the dressing in which to roll both meat and fish, specially trout, before cooking "to give it a quicker relish," wrote Parkinson, in the 17th century.

FLOWERS

The fresh petals of such wholesome flowers as Roses, Marigolds, Chrysanthemums, Sweet Peas and the whole blooms of Anchusa, Borage, Bergamot, Dandelion, Nasturtium, Lavender, Sage, Rosemary etc., contribute much to the pleasure of a salad. They should be strewn or arranged on top just before serving so that they appear quite fresh and tempting. Or they may be chopped fine as a colourful festive garnish.

Any dish when garnished with a few fresh flowers is made more inviting, whether it be fish, meat, cold poultry, game or vegetable. Fresh flowers are admirable too on many sweet dishes, particularly fruit salads.

CANDIED AND CRYSTALLIZED

Flowers and some herbs, especially Angelica and some of the Mints, are invaluable for making edible posies and sprays on iced cakes, cream puddings, trifles, blancmanges, charlotte russes, jellies, etc., or they may be served as they used to be in little sweetmeat dishes. The candying process is worth the trouble.

ANGELICA

Should be candied in late spring using the thick, tender flowering-stems before the flowers open, as well as the thickest leaf-stems. Cut them into 3- or 4-inch lengths. Simmer the sticks till tender with very little water in a closed pan. Peel them and boil again till they are green, then dry them with a cloth.

Allow 1 lb. of sugar to a pound of stalks, mix them and leave them to stand 2 days in a covered earthen jar. Then boil until clear and a good green colour, place them in a colander to drain. Strew on as much fine sugar as will stick to the Angelica and let it dry (not harden) in a cool oven.

ROSE PETALS

Or any edible flowers or leaves may be crystallized quite easily in the following manner:

Gather the petals or flowers during a dry weather spell after the dew has evaporated. Clean them carefully, then dip them into very thin royal icing prepared from the white of an egg well whisked to a stiff froth, and sufficient icing sugar to mix; it should be thin enough to drain off easily. The icing should be coloured and flavoured to suit the particular petals, flowers and leaves, with vegetable colourings and flavourings such as rose water, orange flower water, violet essence, oil of spearmint, and lemon for Balm leaves. Place the dipped and coated petals, etc., on a wire tray and before the icing sets sprinkle them with castor sugar, then let them dry in a very cool oven with the door open.

Anchusa, Borage, Lilac, Sweet Peas, Violets, Orange and Lemon blossoms, are among the edible flowers that may be preserved in this way. The fresh green leaves of Violets, the various Mints and Balm, make tasty leaves for the crystallized floral arrangements.

Rose petals may also be candied or crystallized, by those venturesome enough to try an authentic old method, in the following manner:

Gather the Roses during a dry weather spell, after the dew has evaporated. Have ready dissolved 2 oz. of gum arabic in ½ pint of water. Separate the petals and spread them on a dish. Sprinkle them with the gum solution using only as many petals as it will cover. Spread them on sheets of white paper and sprinkle with castor sugar, then leave them to dry for 24 hours.

Make a syrup with 1 lb. of sugar and ½ pint of water, stirring until the sugar is dissolved, then boil it to a thread degree when tested, colour it with cochineal or carmine. Put the Rose petals into shallow dishes and pour the syrup over them and leave them to soak for 24 hours. Spread out on wire trays and dry them in a cool oven with the door ajar.

MINT LEAVES, OTHER LEAVES, AND PETALS

Can be more simply candied by dipping them in a stiffly beaten egg-white, flavoured with a drop of oil of Spearmint or other suitable flavourings, then coated with castor sugar and dried in a very cool oven with the door open.

POSIES AND SPRAYS INSIDE JELLIES

Can be effectively arranged with a little practice, patience, a bright clear jelly, and a plain mould, bearing in mind that the arrangement is composed upside down to allow for turning out the jelly.

First pour some jelly an inch deep into the mould, let it set on ice. Then put the flowers and leaves in place, pour on more jelly (not hot) to support them. Set it. Add more to the arrangement, with jelly support, until it is built up.

Jellies for this purpose should be very stiff and when the packet types are used they should be dissolved with a little less water than is given in the instructions. More gelatine should be allowed than advised for the "old-fashioned" sorts. And during the building up intervals the unused jelly should be kept in a warm place to prevent its setting.

Single sprays look well and are easy to manage; such as Borage, Anchusa, Comfrey, Lily of the Valley, Violet—in pale coloured lemon jelly. A Nasturtium or two, or Marigolds, make a richly coloured ornament in orange jelly. Leaf sprays of Pineapple or Eau-de-Cologne Mints are good with fruits like dessert gooseberries, strawberries, cherries, currants, which make these set-pieces very inviting.

A pencilled plan of the arrangement should be drawn and turned upside down to work from.

FORCEMEAT

For turkey, veal, fowl, hare, pheasant, etc., this forcemeat, made from an excellent old-fashioned recipe, contains 2 oz. of ham or bacon cut fine, $\frac{1}{4}$ lb. of suet, 6 oz. of breadcrumbs, 2 eggs. To this mixture is added a good tablespoonful of minced Parsley and a heaped teaspoonful of mixed herbs, Lemon Thyme and Marjoram predominating, with a pinch of Common Thyme and a pinch of Winter Savory.

This mixture may be used as stuffing or made into balls and roasted with any game.

MINTY STUFFING OR FORCEMEAT

With a slightly Minty flavour is made with $\frac{1}{4}$ lb. of breadcrumbs, 1 oz. of butter, 1 egg, salt and cayenne pepper to taste. It is flavoured with 6 leaves of Costmary, minced, 2 teaspoonfuls of minced Parsley, ½ dessertspoonful of minced Chives and ¼ teaspoonful of Thyme.

This stuffing is particularly good with veal.

FRITTERS

Both savoury and sweet can be given all sorts of appetizing variations by the addition of herbs. The same batter is used for either type. For a good basic mixture, allow 1 oz. of melted butter to 6 oz. of flour, a pinch of salt and the yolk of an egg. Add about a dessertspoonful of finely chopped or minced herbs, then mix together with a wooden spoon, adding at intervals a teacupful of tepid water. Mix until creamy, then let the batter stand for an hour. When ready to use it, fold in the firmly whisked egg-white.

SAVOURY FRITTERS

May have Sage with grated Shallots or chopped Chives to accompany bacon, ham or pork, etc. Marjoram and Lemon Thyme with beef or ham roll. Fennel, Dill, Parsley, Tarragon, Chervil are especially good to accompany fish. All herbs are worth trying to find the flavours that you yourself find the most satisfying.

SWEET FRITTERS

Are made with the same batter as savoury ones, but it is more delicately flavoured, and they are served with sugar sprinkled over them. The flavours of Caraway seeds, Balm or Basil complement apple fritters, and a few finely-chopped or minced leaves of Rosemary or Eau-de-Cologne Mint are exciting with orange or banana fritters. Mint, especially Pineapple Mint, is pleasant with either apple or pineapple fritters.

COMFREY FRITTERS

Are delicious. Just dip the leaves in cold water, shake them and plunge them into batter, then into sizzling fat in a frying-pan.

GAME AND POULTRY

There are certain herbs which associate most happily with each kind:

HARE: Sage, Bay, Lemon and Common Thymes.
GROUSE AND PIGEON: Parsley, Shallot, Sage, Thymes.
CHICKEN BOILED: Marjoram, Lemon Thyme, Savory, Sorrel, Tarragon.
CHICKEN ROASTED: Rosemary, Lavender, Tarragon, Thymes.
DUCK: Rosemary, Sage, Sorrel, Chives.
GOOSE: Sage, Thymes, Costmary, Shallot, Sorrel, Chives.
PARTRIDGE: Basil, Rosemary.
PHEASANT: Bay, Basil, Marjoram, Oregano.
TURKEY: Basil, Sage, Lemon and Common Thymes.

ICES

Lemon or Orange water ices, or "Sorbets," may be flavoured with fresh herbs, not dried, and served either as a deliciously refreshing interlude during a grand dinner after a rich course, or at the end of a summer or winter meal which does not require a substantial pudding.

For 4 to 6 portions of sorbet, make a syrup with 4 oz. of sugar and ½ pint of water, boiled and stirred until the sugar is thoroughly dissolved. For Lemon Sorbet, add a spray of Pineapple Mint, Mint, or Apple Mint, and allow it to infuse as the syrup cools. When cold, remove the Mint and add ¾ of a cupful of cold water, the juice and grated rind of a large lemon, stir it well and place the mixture in the ice-compartment of the refrigerator, until about an hour before wanted. Whip an egg-white to stiff froth and fold this into the syrup, and return it to the ice-chamber to chill. Serve with the froth on top in suitable glasses; Victorian custard, jelly or ice-cream glasses are ideal.

Orange Sorbet is made in exactly the same way as lemon, but Eau-de-Cologne Mint is used instead of the other varieties.

It is useful that a quantity of the syrup for these ices may be stored for 2 or 3 weeks in a closed jar; also the mixture of syrup and juice can be kept in the refrigerator for several days, but the whisked egg-white should be added only a short time before serving.

JAMS

ROSE-PETAL JAM

Used to be a great delicacy and is still made by certain monks in England, to the delight of foreign visitors.

The best Roses for this are the Cabbage Rose or any of the old ones recommended for herb gardens. For a simple method of making the jam, dry ½ lb. of petals in a shady place. Make a syrup of ½ lb. of white sugar with just enough Rose-water to dissolve it. Then scald the petals in boiling water for a few seconds only. Drain and dry them, then put them into the syrup with 1 dessertspoonful of Orange-Flower water. Boil the mixture until it sets when tested, and pot when cool.

ANGELICA AND RHUBARB

Is a much better flavoured jam than Rhubarb alone. Cut up 4 lb. of Rhubarb and 1 lb. of Angelica stems and put them into a bowl, cover with 4 lb. of sugar and leave for 8 hours. Then put the mixture into a preserving-pan and boil until the jam sets when tested.

APPLE AND MINT JAM

To eat with cold meats such as lamb, mutton or pork.

Wash the apples and cut in half, put them into a preserving-pan with enough water nearly to cover them. Simmer until quite soft and then rub through a sieve. Return the pulp to the preserving-pan in a pint measure, and for each pint allow ¾ lb. of sugar. Add a large bunch of freshly gathered Mint and boil until the jam sets when tested. Remove the Mint before potting. This jam requires to be strongly flavoured with Mint otherwise it is insipid.

ELDER-BERRY JELLY

Remove the Elder-berries from the stalks and boil them with half their measure of water. When soft and pulpy, strain slowly through a hair-sieve. Make separately an equal amount of apple or blackberry juice. When all the juice is strained, mix together and add 1 lb. of hot sugar to each pint and boil until the jelly sets when tested.

JELLIES

Made with herbs are so delicious to eat with cold meats and in sandwiches that a store of them should be made and kept in a cool, dry place. July is the best time to make them as the herbs are then most strongly flavoured. Here are some good old recipes.

MINT JELLY

For lamb and other meats. Chop up 6 lb. of green apples and cook them to a pulp with just enough water to draw the juice and prevent them burning. Strain the juice through a hair-sieve. Boil the liquid for 15 minutes before adding 2¼ lb. of sugar, the juice of 4 lemons and ¼ pint of white wine vinegar. Stir till the sugar is dissolved then add a large bunch of fresh Mint. Boil until a good Mint flavour is imparted, adding more Mint if necessary. Then remove the herb and colour the liquid green with a good vegetable dye. As soon as the jelly sets when tried on a cold saucer, pot it in small jars, and seal when cold.

Made another way. Pick and clean the fresh Mint leaves, strip them from the stalks when perfectly dry. To every cupful of leaves, allow ½ cupful of castor sugar. Keep them separate and chop finely or mince the Mint leaves. To every ½ cupful of sugar allow ½ oz. of powdered gelatine, ½ cupful of good vinegar and 1 lemon. Melt the gelatine in water, allowing 1 cupful to a ½ oz. Add the strained juice of the lemon, then stir in the vinegar. Add the sugar and stir until dissolved. Stir in the chopped Mint and bring to boil then simmer for 10 to 15 minutes, or until it jellies when tested on a cold saucer. When it is ready, add a few drops of green colouring. Pot in small jars and seal when cold.

PARSLEY JELLY

Fill a preserving-pan with fresh Parsley leaves and barely cover them with water. Simmer for ½ hour, then strain. To every pint of liquid add the juice of a large lemon and the thinly peeled rind, and 1 lb. of sugar. Return to the pan and boil until the jelly sets when tested on a cold saucer. Pot in small jars and cover when cold.

SAGE JELLY

Is made as Parsley Jelly or as the Mint Jelly with gelatine.

LAVENDER JELLY

Made as Mint Jelly with gelatine is an ancient and delicious delicacy — try it with cold lamb!

JELLIES FOR DESSERT

Both lemon and orange dessert jellies may be pleasantly flavoured with herbs. Here are two old recipes which should please those diners, or invalids, who prefer the elegant old-fashioned delicacies to the modern packet type. Both herbs could as well be used with these "squares."

LEMON JELLY

Peel 2 big juicy lemons thinly, place the peel in a pan with 1 pt. of cold water, 1½ oz. of powdered gelatine, 6 oz. of sugar and a dessertspoonful of Coriander seeds. Stir till the sugar is dissolved then bring just to the boil. Remove the pan from the heat and put the lid on for a few minutes to infuse flavours. Then add the lemon juice and a wineglassful of sherry and strain through a hot jelly-bag, or fine cloth, into a mould.

Lemon jelly may be deliciously enriched with a spray of Pineapple Mint instead of Coriander seeds.

ORANGE JELLY

Can be made in the same way as the Lemon Jelly, using a very large juicy orange or 2 small ones, and instead of Coriander seeds a spray of Eau-de-Cologne Mint, which should be removed before the jelly is strained.

MEAT

All herbs can be used with meat dishes but some are particularly good with certain kinds, and for their subtle or distinctive flavours to be properly enjoyed they should be chosen according to the type of meat and the method of cooking.

BEEF ROASTED: May be rubbed with Thyme, Marjoram or Rosemary and Lavender, and carry a sprig or two into the oven. In past times *Thymus Herba-barona* was rubbed over "Baron of Beef" to contribute its pleasantly pungent, slightly Caraway flavour to that noble joint, and it does as well for commoner cuts today.

LAMB, MUTTON AND BEEF ROASTED: May be garnished ready for cooking with a sprinkling of Rosemary, Lavender or a leaf or two of Bay. And the mild Garlic flavour from a few spikes of that herb inserted with a knife point into the skin and around the bone generally titillates the appetite for a leg of lamb, of mutton or a joint of beef.

BEEF MINCE is most effectively flavoured with Chervil, Marjoram, Oregano, Savory and Chives.

BEEF STEW: Can take a small spray of the pungent Hyssop, and Balm, Basil, Chervil, Marjoram, Rosemary, Lavender, Sweet Cicely and Coriander seeds and leaves.

BEEF STEAK: Is enriched with Parsley and Marjoram.

LAMB CHOPS OR CUTLETS: May have Basil, Dill and Marjoram.

LAMB STEW: Has the wide choice of Marjoram, Bay, Chervil, Costmary, Parsley, Rosemary, Lavender, Thymes and a leaf or two of Coriander.

HAM ROAST OR BOILED: Basil, Dill and Marjoram.

PORK CHOPS: Dill and Marjoram.

PORK ROASTED: Has the wide choice of Basil, Caraway, Dill, Lemon Thyme, Sage, Marjoram, Oregano, Rosemary, Lavender and Savory.

VEAL CUTLETS: Chervil, Parsley and Costmary.

VEAL ROAST: Basil, Marjoram, Oregano, Rosemary, Tarragon, Thymes and Costmary.

RISSOLES: Parsley, Chives, Marjoram, Basil; any herbs are suitable according to the meat and personal taste.

SAUSAGES: Are improved by a mixture of herbs added to the meat. Basil predominated in the flavouring of the once famous "Fetter Lane" sausages.

TRIPE: That easily digested nourishing meat seldom appears in cookery books with its Sage flavouring. During the latter half of the 19th century, it became a popular supper-dish served at several fashionable London restaurants, and it should be enjoyed today by following this favourite old recipe.

Peel and cut up two onions, place them in cold water with a good pinch of salt and boil for 3 minutes, strain them and put into a pan. Cut 1½ lb. of tripe into 4 inch pieces and place them on the onions with the finely peeled rind of half a lemon, a few Sage leaves and a small bunch of Lemon Thyme. Add 1 pint of milk and 1 pint of water. Stew slowly till tender, then make a thickening with 1 oz. butter, 2 good tablespoonfuls of flour, salt and pepper to taste, and mix with the liquor from the tripe until it is smooth and creamy. Then add ½ teacupful of cream. Return to the tripe and mix together. Serve hot with small pieces of toast, fried sausages and baked or mashed potatoes.

PASTRY

Such things as patties, savoury flans, etc., can be given all sorts of exciting flavours by mixing finely chopped or minced herbs into the dough before rolling out. The herbs should be chosen according to the filling that is to be used, for instance, Tarragon and Chives, Basil and Parsley, Lemon Thyme and Marjoram, are all good partners for cheese fillings, and for minced or chopped poultry or meat, also for fish fillings. Mint-flavoured cases add zest to bacon and egg flans.

PICKLES

All kinds of herbs, particularly Garlic and Bay, appear in pickling recipes, and Dill seed is the necessary ingredient for the most delicious methods of pickling cucumbers. The following recipe is from the *Receipt Book* of Joseph Cooper, cook to King Charles I, 1640, and it is still excellent, especially the latter part using white wine vinegar.

PICKLED CUCUMBER WITH DILL

"Gather the tops of the ripest Dill and cover the bottom of a vessel, and lay a layer of cucumbers and a layer of Dill till you have filled the vessel within a handful of the top. Then take as much water as you think will fill the vessel and mix it with salt and a quarter of a pound of allom (alum) to a gallon of water and poure it on them and press them down with a stone on them and keep them covered close. For that use I think the water will be best boyl'd and cold, which will keep longer sweet, or if you like not this pickle, doe it with water, salt and white wine vinegar, or (if you please) poure the water and salt on them scalding hot which will make them ready to use the sooner."

PICKLED CUCUMBERS WITH DILL AND FENNEL

Are excellent. If the cucumbers are young and very small they may be used whole, but large ones should be cut into pieces about 2 inches long. Put them into an earthenware pan and sprinkle with coarse salt. Let them stand for 24 hours. Pour off the liquid and wipe them with a clean cloth. Return to dried pan. Boil the vinegar allowing per quart a few peppercorns, a blade of mace, a Bay leaf and 1 oz. of salt. Pour the hot vinegar over the Cucumbers and leave 24 hours. Then pour it off and boil again, repeating the process 3 times. After the third time, when cold, place in a large storage jar (confectioners' large glass sweet jars are ideal) a layer of Dill and Fennel—chopped stalks, leaves and seed-heads—a layer of cucumbers covered with another of Dill and Fennel, until the jar is filled, then pour in the cool vinegar, seal the jar tightly, and store in a dry cool place. White wine vinegar makes the sharpest pickle.

DILL AND COLLYFLOWER PICKLE

From *Acetaria, a book about Sallets* (1680), by John Evelyn:

"Boil the Collyflowers till they fall in pieces; then with some of the stalk and worst of the flower boil it in a part of the liquer till pretty strong. Then being taken off strain it; and when settled, clean it from the bottom. Then with Dill, gross pepper, a pretty quantity of salt, when cold add as much vinegar as will make it sharp and pour all upon the Collyflower."

NASTURTIUM SEEDS FOR IMITATION CAPERS

Gather the seeds soon after the flowers have fallen. Fill a jar with them and add salt water to cover. Let them soak for 3 days, changing the brine each day. Drain them and dry in a cloth, then return them to the empty jar in layers with a few Tarragon leaves and grated horseradish between them. Boil for 10 minutes as much white wine vinegar as you need to cover the seeds (this amount can be discovered by measuring the salt water used), add to this in proportion, to each pint allow 1 sliced shallot, 1 oz. of salt, 12 peppercorns, a blade of mace and a dash of nutmeg. When cold, strain it over the seeds and cover them closely.

PICKLED ELDER SHOOTS LIKE INDIAN PICKLE

From Elizabeth Raffald's *English Housekeeper* (1814).

"Gather your elder shoots when they are the thickness of a pipe shank (in May), put them into salt water all night, then put them into stone jars in layers, and betwixt every layer strew a little mustard seed, and scraped horseradish, a few shallots, a little white beet root, and cauliflowers cut in small pieces, then pour boiling alegar (malt vinegar) upon it, and scald it three times, and it will be like piccalillo, or Indian Pickle; tie a leather over it, and keep it in a dry place."

PICKLED ELDER SHOOTS IN IMITATION OF INDIAN BAMBOO

Another old recipe advised the cutting in May of thick, tender, young shoots from the middle of the bushes, selecting only the greenest. Each piece must be carefully chosen as it must not be too immature, and not at all woody.

Peel off all outer skin and lay them in salt water overnight. Next morning, prepare the pickle for Mock Bamboo.

To a quart of vinegar, add 1 oz. of white pepper, 1 oz. of ginger, a small blade of mace, and boil all well together. Remove the Elder shoots from the salt and water, dry in a cloth and slice up into suitable pieces, laying them in a stone (or glass) jar. Pour the boiling mixture over them and either place them in an oven for 2 hours, or in a pan of boiling water on the stove. When cold the pickle should be green in colour. If not, strain the liquor, boil it up again, pour over the shoots and repeat the process. To retain the essence of the plant, the jar must be kept completely airtight.

PUDDINGS

RICE PUDDING AND CORNFLOUR SHAPE

Used to be given a pleasant aromatic flavour with a Bay leaf.

The gingerish Tansy was once the herb most fancied for flavouring puddings, especially those served at Easter, as Tansy was particularly associated with that festival. But the taste was so popular that Tansy puddings were made whenever the fresh herb was available. Two ancient recipes give delicious results.

TANSY PANCAKES

Beat 2 eggs, add ¼ pint of cream (or top milk), 2 tablespoonfuls of flour, 1 oz. of castor sugar. Beat together very well then add a teaspoonful of Tansy juice with a dash of nutmeg. Beat again and fry as pancakes in a pan greased with butter. Serve hot garnished with sections of orange and dredged with castor sugar.

TANSY PUDDING OF GROUND RICE

Boil 3 oz. of ground rice in a pint of milk until it is soft. Then add ¼ lb. of butter and 3 well-beaten eggs, sugar and rose-water to taste. Beat some spinach (to colour) and a few Tansy leaves in a mortar. Squeeze out the juice through a cloth and mix well to the mixture. Pour into a buttered dish and bake gently about ¾ of an hour. When you dish it up stick it all over with half quarters of orange.

MINT PASTY

An old North of England pleasure is made with fresh Mint finely chopped or minced, brown sugar and currants in equal quantities, with a knob of butter mixed and pounded then spread between layers of rich pastry, and baked until the top paste is golden colour.

ELDER-FLOWERS

With their subtle muscatel flavour were once considerably important in fine cookery. Stripped from their green stems, the blossoms were beaten up in batters for flannel cakes, muffins and pancakes, to give their delicate taste and improve the texture of the batter.

ELDER-FLOWER PANCAKES

Are delicious and made by dipping the flat-topped mass of creamy fragrant blossoms into a light batter and frying them, then dusting them with castor sugar.

ELDER-FLOWER MILK

A rare delicacy, is created with stalkless flowers from at least 2 large clusters, simmered for 10 minutes in 2 pints of milk. Then a tablespoonful of semolina is added and beaten into the milk with a pinch of salt, 2 egg-yolks and sugar to taste. When cool the mixture is poured into a bowl and little islands of the egg-whites, stiffly whipped with a little castor sugar, are floated on top and the whole surface is sprinkled with castor sugar and ground-cinnamon.

SALADS

Any sort of salad mixed without some enticing herb flavours can be a comparatively dull thing. Some edible flowers, too, make a salad invitingly festive, and they have delicate pleasant flavours and definite health-giving qualities.

A heaped tablespoonful of mixed herbs is about enough for an ordinary-sized mixed green salad. The flavours should be carefully blended by using only very small quantities, and finely chopped, of some of the more potent leaves such as Rue, Savory, Marjoram, Lavender, Basil, Bergamot, Rosemary, Hyssop, Sage, Tarragon, Coriander, Costmary, the several Thymes and Mints, Balm, Chives.

The more delicately-flavoured leaves may be coarsely cut and they can be generously used according to personal taste. These are the cucumberish-tasting young shoots and leaves of Borage and Salad Burnet; Nasturtium which is pleasantly acid and like its close relation Water Cress; the vitamin-packed familiar Parsley and celery-flavoured Lovage. Dandelion leaves are too often neglected, but from plants grown in goodish soil they are excellent in salads, resembling chicory or endive in their bitterish taste. They actually contain 4 times more vitamin C than lettuce, are rich in vitamin A, in potassium, and their iron content is greater than that of spinach. In France these health-giving plants are specially grown and marketed for salads.

Neglected, too, are the fleshy leaves of Purslane which when stripped of their tough stems are as good today and as nutty-flavoured as they were long ago when they were more popular than lettuce. Numerous 17th- and 18th-century recipes survive for Purslane's uses. Giles Rose, a master cook to Charles II, left us his receipt for "Sallets of lettice and Purslan": "Take of the newest Purslan, pick and wash it very well, swing it out and land it round of the plate and lettice round about it, garnish the brim with Chervil and Flowers of divers colours, very small."

Garlic can be an improvement to any salad when it is liked. For those who prefer a mere suggestion of this potent herb it should be either rubbed around the bowl or rubbed on a piece of dry bread and placed in the bowl before the salad is mixed, so it may but breathe on the whole content. But, for the hardy who relish this distinctive flavour, a finely-chopped clove or two may be mixed into the salad, or a few drops of the juice may be squeezed by an extractor either into the salad or the dressing. A little Garlic vinegar in a dressing should quite convert the doubtful to favour its merits as a titillating relish to most salads.

Sorrel leaves roughly cut are a very refreshing salad herb.

Some herbs are particularly good for blending with certain kinds or salad and for the best results it is useful to know the range of complementary flavours so that the ones preferred may be used either singly of in a mixture of 2 or 3 or more if desired.

APPLE AND BEETROOT SALAD: Capers or Nasturtium seeds, fresh or pickled. Sorrel, Water Cress.

ASPARAGUS SALAD: Parsley, Tarragon, Chervil.

AVOCADO PEAR SALAD: Marjoram, Oregano.

BEAN SALAD: Parsley, Chives, Sorrel.

BEETROOT AND CUCUMBER SALAD: Tarragon, Parsley, Chives.

BEETROOT SALAD: Mint, Chives, Parsley.

BROAD BEAN SALAD: Summer or Winter Savory, Parsley, Lemon Thyme.

CABBAGE AND APPLE COLESLAW: Caraway, Dill, Poppy seeds.

CABBAGE SALAD: Chives, Caraway, Dill, Marjoram, Poppy seeds, Nasturtium leaves, seeds and flowers, Lovage, Water Cress, Sorrel.

CARROT SALAD: Anise, Parsley, Mint, Marjoram, Thyme, Chives, Bay, Sweet Cicely.

CAULIFLOWER SALAD: Mint, Parsley.

CELERIAC AND POTATO SALAD: Parsley, Bay, Thyme, Sorrel, Water Cress.

CHEESE AND TOMATO SALAD: Chives, Parsley, Nasturtium, Water Cress.

CUCUMBER SALAD: Dill, Chives, Nasturtium, Fennel, Water Cress.

DANDELION SALAD: Parsley, Chives, Garlic, Borage, etc.

EGG SALAD : Chives, Parsley, Thymes, Tarragon, Sorrel, Water Cress.

ENDIVE SALAD : Garlic, Parsley, Chives, Sorrel, Water Cress.

FISH SALAD : Fennel, Dill, Parsley, Chives, Chervil, Water Cress.

LETTUCE SALAD : Parsley, Chives, Tarragon, Mint, Chervil, Lavender.

MIXED GREEN SALAD : Most herbs, and Coriander seed and leaves, also the seeds of Caraway, Dill and Poppy.

NASTURTIUM AND CUCUMBER SALAD : the flowers, Fennel, Dill and Poppy seeds.

POTATO SALAD : Chives, Dill, Caraway, Parsley, Mint, Garlic, Savory, Sweet Cicely, Sorrel, Water Cress.

RAW VEGETABLE SALAD : Chives, Parsley, Lovage, Lavender, Savory, Sorrel, Water Cress, Poppy seeds, etc.

TOMATO AND LETTUCE SALAD : Parsley, Chervil, Tarragon, Basil, Savory.

TOMATO SALAD : Basil, Parsley, Chives, Oregano, Tarragon, Savory.

WATER CRESS AND APPLE SALAD : Fennel, Dill, Marjoram.

FRUIT SALAD : the various Mints, Balm, a leaf or two of Coriander and the seeds of Caraway and Coriander.

SAUCES

Flavoured with herbs, these are often cleverly designed not only to enhance the dish they accompany but to make it more easily digested, as Mint Sauce with lamb, an immature meat and difficult to digest, and Fennel Sauce which corrects the indigestibility of fish oils, especially salmon, mackerel and herrings. These herbs should be generously used in sauces.

SAVOURY SAUCES

Offer scope for experimenting with herb flavours and it may be useful to be reminded of some excellent recipes and the herbs used to give them distinction.

ALMOND SAUCE

For cold fish.

Pound till smooth ½ oz. of ground sweet almonds and 1 oz. of blanched pistachio nuts. Work in a dessertspoonful of cold white sauce and rub through a sieve. Add 3 egg yolks beaten, ½ teaspoonful of salt and ½ teaspoonful of ground pepper. Beat well and mix in 1 pint of olive oil and the juice of a lemon. Finish with 1½ tablespoonfuls of finely chopped or minced herbs, Parsley, Tarragon, Chervil and Chives.

ANISETTE SAUCE

For cold lobster.

Shell 1 pint of shrimps and add them to a dressing sauce of olive oil, vinegar, a little made mustard and chopped or minced herbs, Parsley, Tarragon, Chervil and Chives. Season with salt and pepper to taste. Add the juice of half a lemon and finish with a wineglassful of anisette.

BÉCHAMEL SAUCE WITH HERBS

Put ½ pint of milk and ½ pint of good stock into a saucepan with a shallot, a bouquet of Thyme, Parsley and a Bay leaf, 6 peppercorns, and a blade of mace, with salt and pepper to taste. Bring to boil slowly. Make a roux with 1½ oz. of butter and 1 oz. of flour, add the liquid and whisk until it boils, then simmer for 20 minutes. Strain and serve hot.

DILL SAUCE

From Switzerland, for fish dishes.

Make a roux with 1 oz. of butter and 1 oz. of flour, moisten with ¼ pint of cream and stir until perfectly smooth. Boil a pint of veal or other good stock and add it gradually to the creamed mixture. Add 2 tablespoonfuls of chopped Dill. Simmer for 15 minutes, preferably in a double saucepan as it must not boil.

FENNEL AND PARSLEY

Chopped into melted butter make an excellent sauce for boiled fish.

FENNEL SAUCE

For boiled salmon, mackerel or any fish. Add a generous amount of coarsely-chopped Fennel to a good white sauce, and do not let it boil after the herb has been added.

For casseroled fish steaks or fillets. Place the fish in a casserole with a slice of butter and close tightly. When cooked, about 30 minutes in a moderate oven, put a dessertspoonful of flour into a saucepan and mix in the liquor from the fish making a smooth sauce, adding a little top milk and salt and pepper to taste. When it is creamy add 2 good tablespoonfuls of coarsely-chopped Fennel.

For boiled mutton. A sprig of Fennel should be boiled with the meat. Make a good white sauce with a tablespoonful of butter and 2 table-spoonfuls of flour, moistened with ¾ pint of the meat stock. Cook for 10 minutes then add 1½ tablespoonfuls of white wine vinegar, 2 teaspoon-fuls of sugar and 2 tablespoonfuls of coarsely-chopped Fennel. Stir until mixed then bind the sauce with an egg yolk.

TARRAGON SAUCE

For boiled fowl or rabbit.

Put into a saucepan ½ pint of milk and ½ pint of stock from the fowl or rabbit, with a shallot and a handful of chopped Tarragon leaves. Season with salt and cayenne pepper to taste. Bring to boil. Make a roux with 1½ oz. of butter and 1 oz. of flour. Add the liquid and whisk until it boils, then simmer for a few minutes and serve hot.

PARSLEY AND TARRAGON SAUCE

For boiled fowl or rabbit served hot or cold.

Boil ½ pint of milk and ½ teacupful of stock from the boiled meat, with a thin strip of lemon rind. Make a roux with ½ oz. of butter and 1 table-spoonful of flour, mix in a little lemon juice, ½ teaspoonful of made mustard, 1 teaspoonful of mayonnaise, season with salt and pepper to taste. Add the milk and stock gradually and a heaped tablespoonful of chopped Parsley or Tarragon or both, stirring until the sauce is smooth and creamy.

TOMATO CREAM SAUCE (AMERICAN)

For white fish, cutlets, beef, spaghetti, macaroni.

Stew 2 breakfastcupfuls of chopped tomatoes for 20 minutes with a spray of Thyme, 2 Lovage leaves, 1 shallot or 2 tablespoonfuls of Chives and a small Bay leaf. Salt and pepper to taste. Then rub through a sieve, stir in a good pinch of bicarbonate of soda to prevent curdling, and add a breakfastcupful of thick white sauce. Mix together till smooth.

TOMATO SAUCE (ITALIAN)

Used for the same dishes as the American Tomato Sauce. To make it, boil together 8 ripe tomatoes sliced, 1 tablespoonful of chopped Chives, 2 Lovage leaves, a few leaves of Basil, a spray of Thyme and a bunch of Parsley. Add ½ cupful of pure olive oil, a pinch of salt, and a dash of pepper. Cook, stirring until thick and creamy, then strain and serve hot.

SORREL SAUCE

Wash and cook 1 lb. of Sorrel in a sauce-pan with 1 oz. of butter and the moisture from the washed leaves. Add 8 gooseberries when they are in season. Keep turning it with a wooden spoon to prevent burning. When tender, rub through a wire sieve to a purée and mix this with an equal quantity of the gravy; season to taste.

SEASONINGS

MUSTARD

Is an ancient medicinal and salad herb whose seeds have provided a condiment from earliest times. A little of Mustard seed's culinary history may be useful to suggest ideas for exploring their possibilities as a pleasurable seasoning.

The Greeks liked Mustard, and the Romans were particularly fond of the seeds pounded with new wine. The Saxons ate them any way; and to judge from historical references to Mustard its popularity never waned. Tussor mentioned the plants being cultivated in gardens. And at an early date the seeds were ground at Tewkesbury; Shakespeare referred to Tewkesbury Mustard in *Henry IV*. In 1657 Coles, the herbalist, said: "In Glostershire about Teuxbury they grind Mustard seed and make it up into balls which are brought to London and other remote places as being the best that the world affords." Gerard wrote: "The seeds of Mustard pounded with vinegar is an excellent sauce."

The Mustard condiment of olden days was usually made with the pure black and white seeds pounded together, the powder was made into balls with honey, a little cinnamon, and moistened with vinegar. These were stored till wanted, then they were reduced with more vinegar, often a herbal one.

At the end of the 18th century, a Mrs. Clements of Durham invented a method of preparing Mustard powder. After removing the husks, she put the seeds through rollers, then pounded them in a mortar. But adulterations with a farinaceous substitute, coloured with turmeric, were made by many manufacturers.

John Evelyn recommended "best Tewkesbury" or the "soundest and weightiest Yorkshire seeds" for making Mustard. He also said the Italians mixed orange and lemon peel with black Mustard seed.

CONTINENTAL MUSTARD

Of which the best came from Dijon, was flavoured with various spices, Anchovies, Capers, Tarragon and catsup of Mushrooms or Walnuts.

HERB MUSTARD

Is good made from pounded seeds or a reliable proprietary brand of Mustard powder, mixed with a pinch of herb salt, a sprinkle of herb pepper and a little olive oil, then reduced with any of the herb vinegars.

MILD HERB MUSTARD

Can be mixed with a little cream, a pinch of herb salt and a few drops of Tarragon vinegar.

MUSTARD WITH DRIED HERBS

May be created in various flavours by blending a pinch of the dried herb with the Mustard powder, and mixing with the matching vinegar. As a suggestion, try Sage or Thyme with duck, goose or pork; Tarragon with fowl, etc.; Rosemary or Lavender with lamb; Garlic or Chives with beef.

HERB PEPPER

Is made from dried and powdered herbs. To $\frac{1}{4}$ oz. each of black and white pepper, and $\frac{1}{2}$ oz. of powdered mace, a pinch of allspice or cinnamon, add $\frac{1}{2}$ oz. each of Rosemary, Marjoram, Black Thyme and Winter Savory. Sieve the mixture and bottle it for use.

HERB SALT

Is a mixture of 1 part herb pepper to 4 parts of salt.

SOUPS

The most suitable herbs for flavouring soups may be listed according to the soup's ingredients.

CHICKEN: Chervil, Balm, Lavender, Rosemary, Tarragon, Parsley, Lemon Thyme, Lovage, Sorrel.

FISH: Bay, Chervil, Dill, Fennel, Parsley, Savory, Thyme, Garlic.

MEAT: Balm, Basil, Bay, Chervil, Chives, Marjoram, Sorrel, Lavender, Rosemary, Parsley, Coriander seeds and leaves, Hyssop may be used sparingly, a leaf or two only, to add its warm flavour, and Sweet Cicely and Lovage leaves give a full rich taste.

LENTIL: Winter Savory, Lovage, Chervil, Sorrel.

MUSHROOM: Fennel, Parsley, Tarragon.

ONION: Marjoram, Sage, Thymes.

PEA: Costmary, Mint, Parsley, Tarragon, Thymes, Savory.

POTATO: Dill, Marjoram, Mint, Parsley, Water Cress or Nasturtium.

TOMATO: Basil, Rosemary, Lavender, Oregano, Marjoram, Parsley, Tarragon, Thymes, Chives, Water Cress or Nasturtium.

VEGETABLE: Balm, Bay, Coriander, Marjoram, Parsley, Thymes Lavender, Sweet Cicely, Water Cress, Chervil, Sorrel.

"CHIFFONNADE" GARNISH

For soups is made with one-third chopped Sorrel and two-thirds chopped lettuce leaves, seasoned and cooked in butter on gentle heat.

WATER CRESS SOUP

Is a delicious herb soup liked by everyone.

Wash and dry 2 good bunches of Water Cress, picking out the yellowish leaves. Plunge the stems and leaves into boiling salted water to scald for a moment, then strain it and chop it finely. Put a piece of butter into a saucepan and when it boils add the chopped Cress and turn it about with a wooden spoon for 5 minutes over a slow burner. Stir in a little water if necessary to keep it from burning. Cook 1 tablespoonful of tapioca in 1 pint of water till clear, then add 1 pint of milk and beat them together before adding the Water Cress. Season with salt and pepper to taste. Beat up the yolk of an egg in the soup tureen and add a lump of butter. Before pouring the soup, stir in a small cupful of cream, then pour it over the egg, stirring well to prevent curdling.

Another kind, the French *Velouté Cressonnière*, is made as follows.

Cut and slice 1 lb. of potatoes. Put them into 2½ pints of boiling water and cook. Wash and trim a large bunch of Water Cress, put the stalks to cook with the potatoes. Mix a thickening in the tureen with 2 egg yolks, 3 tablespoonfuls of cream, and 1 oz. of butter. When the potatoes are cooked strain into another saucepan, mashing the potatoes. Bring to the boil again adding the Water Cress leaves. Cook for 3 minutes only. Pour into the tureen stirring in the thickening. Serve with small croûtons fried in butter.

CHERVIL SOUP

Potage Crème Velouté de Cerfeuil.

Trim and wash 1 lb. 2 oz. of Chervil bulbs, boil 2 pints of water, add a little salt and cook the roots 15 minutes, skimming off foam. Press the cooked roots through a sieve for purée. Keep the liquid. Cook ½ oz. of rice flour in 1 gill of milk. Blend this thickening with the purée, add the Chervil water gradually, and re-heat. Mix 3 tablespoonfuls of cream with 2 egg yolks, add 1 oz. of butter cut into small pieces; pour the hot soup over, mix it well and serve, garnished with Chervil leaves and small croûtons fried in butter.

CONSOMMÉ À LA CHIFFONNADE

Warm 2¾ pints of consommé. Wash and cut up a lettuce, a handful of Sorrel, a handful of spinach and a large spoonful of chopped Chervil leaves. Put 1½ oz. of butter in a saucepan with the lettuce and a spoonful of water; cook for 6 minutes, then add the Sorrel and spinach; stir them about to prevent burning for another 6 minutes. Add the cooked herbs to the hot consommé and serve with the Chervil floating on top.

CHERVIL POTAGE

A quickly made recipe from France.

To 1 pint of vegetable stock, or a bouillon cube or meat extract diluted in boiling water, add a small piece of butter. Cut 2 or 3 thin slices of stale bread and spread on them a thick layer of minced or finely-chopped Chervil leaves. Place the bread on the bottom of the tureen, season with salt and pepper; put on 6 tablespoonfuls of cream and pour on the boiling stock.

HERB POTAGE

A very nice soup can be made by adding to a pint of stock or bouillon cube diluted in a pint of boiling water, 2 tablespoonfuls of lentils and the following herbs: a large leaf of Lovage, a leaf of Sweet Cicely, 2 good sprays of Marjoram, a spray of Lemon Thyme, 3 Basil leaves, a Parsley leaf. Boil until the lentils are quite soft.

SORREL SOUP

Potage Velouté à l'Oseille is a favourite French potage and an excellent reviver for the tired and weary.

To make it, first boil $2\frac{1}{2}$ oz. of vermicelli and set aside. Put 2 egg yolks in a tureen and mix them with 3 tablespoonfuls of cream. Whisk up the egg whites. Wash and cut 8 oz. of Sorrel, put 2 oz. of butter into a saucepan with the Sorrel, and, when melted, pour on $\frac{1}{2}$ pint of boiling water, add the whisked egg whites and stir while cooking for a few minutes on low heat; add salt and pepper to taste. Meantime, boil $1\frac{1}{2}$ pints of milk and pour it slowly into the mixture, adding the cooked vermicelli. Pour the smooth potage very hot into the tureen, stirring and mixing with the egg yolk and cream; add 2 oz. of butter before serving very hot.

TEAS

HERB TEAS

Tisanes, in French, are made by infusing fresh or dried herbs with boiling water. The infusions must be kept covered to prevent their health-giving qualities escaping with the steam. Half a pint of water is usually used to cover a handful of fresh leaves or a level teaspoonful of dried herbs. The dosage is half a pint daily of any of the tisanes. They may be made from single herbs or a mixture and taken for comfort or pleasure.

ANGELICA: For colds, coughs, flatulence, rheumatism, or just an aromatic drink.

CORIANDER: Soothing, and a relief for flatulence.

COSTMARY: Anti-spasmodic, astringent and a mild aperient.

BALM: For cooling fevers, influenza, catarrh. Balm tea may be flavoured with lemon and sugar or honey, for a cooling summer drink.

CARAWAY SEEDS: Make a soothing cordial for flatulent indigestion, and it is particularly comforting for infants. Infuse 1 oz. of bruised seeds for 6 hours in cold water. The infusion may be sweetened with honey or sugar. The dose for infants is from 1 to 3 teaspoonfuls.

BERGAMOT: By adding 1 or 2 dried flower-heads of this herb to a pot of ordinary Indian tea, you make an unusually fragrant delicious brew. Fresh heads may be used—freed from lurking insects!

DANDELION: For biliousness. Allow 1 oz. of leaves to 1 pint of boiling water and infuse for 15 minutes.

DILL: Practically identical with Caraway seeds.

HYSSOP: For chest troubles, chronic catarrh and rheumatism. The tea can be made either from fresh green tops, the leaves or flowers fresh or dried. Applications of the green herb, bruised, heal cuts quickly. In America an infusion of the leaves is used externally for relieving muscular rheumatism.

ELDER-FLOWER: A good spring medicine and blood purifier taken for several weeks each morning before breakfasting. It is mildly astringent, a gentle laxative and comforting for colds, influenza, throat troubles and can be used as an eye-bath to relieve inflammation.

MARIGOLD PETALS: Only the common type should be used, allowing 1 oz. of petals to 1 pint of water. This infusion is good for inflamed eyes (as an eye-bath), or is taken as a mild aperient.

MINTS: For nausea and flatulence. Infuse a handful of fresh leaves or 1 oz. of dried leaves with 1 pint of water. Dose, ½ wineglassful when needed. As an aid to digestion, 4 or 5 fresh leaves may be infused in a cupful of boiling water.

PARSLEY: Especially good for rheumatism and liver disorders. This tea is made with a handful of fresh leaves in a pint of cold water, this is brought to the boil then simmered for ½ an hour. A stronger brew is said to be helpful for bladder disorders that cause urine retention.

ROSEMARY: A stomachic and a comfort for nervous headaches.

SAGE: A stomachic, a stimulant and reliever of dyspepsia. Good for colds and as a mouthwash or gargle. A pint of Sage tea may be flavoured with the rind and juice of a lemon.

SWEET CICELY: Is taken for coughs, flatulence and as an appetite reviver for a weak stomach.

THYMES: For colds, catarrh, sore throat and flatulence. Thyme tea may be sweetened with honey.

RUE: A remedy for colic and flatulence. The infusion needs only 3 sprays of Rue leaves to ½ pint of boiling water.

CHAMOMILE: A sedative and relief for headaches and for chest troubles, it is used also to prevent nightmares. Allow 7 dried flower-heads to ½ pint of boiling water. The cup should be covered and the flowers infused for 10 minutes. It may be sweetened.

ANISE: For colds and catarrhs. This tea is particularly good for infants.

BORAGE: A cooling drink for feverish conditions and for relieving pulmonary ailments, also it is effective for promoting kidney activities. It is a really soothing tisane and makes a pleasant cooling drink in hot weather.

LIME FLOWERS: LINDEN TEA, "TILLEUL": Is the most popular of tisanes in France. It has the effect of soothing nervous spasms, palpitation and indigestion. The dried flowers must be reasonably fresh, as if they are too old the tisane can have a bad effect. It may be made from fresh flowers when in season.

VEGETABLES

For all vegetables there are certain herbs whose flavours blend most happily with theirs, either during cooking or in sauce to serve with them, or as a garnish; the choice of use is the cook's, but the choice of herb should be governed to some extent by ancient experience.

ARTICHOKES: Dill, Parsley.

ASPARAGUS: Dill, Caraway, Tarragon, in sauce. Chervil on mayonnaise for cold asparagus.

BEANS, FRESH: Fennel, Oregano, Savory, Sorrel, fresh sprigs of Summer Savory boiled with *broad beans*, and in sauce.

BEANS, DRIED: Basil, Savory, in sauce.

BEETROOT: Tarragon, Thyme, chopped and sprinkled on the cooked beets, or in sauce.

BROCCOLI: Oregano, chopped and sprinkled on the cooked broccoli, or in sauce.

BRUSSELS SPROUTS: Marjoram, chopped and sprinkled over when cooked.

CABBAGE: Caraway, Marjoram, Poppy seeds, Tarragon, any of these may be used to flavour the cooking.

CARROTS: Marjoram, Mint, Oregano, Thyme, chopped in white wine sauce or lemon sauce. Anise may be finely chopped to sprinkle on carrots.

CAULIFLOWER: Marjoram, Savory, Sorrel, chopped in sauce.

CELERY: Bay, Chives, in sauce.

CELERIAC: Parsley, in sauce.

CORN: Chives, Parsley, in sauce.

CUCUMBER: Bay, Coriander, Dill, when raw.

LEEKS: Thyme, Parsley, in sauce.

MARROWS: Parsley in sauce for boiled or braised marrow. Stuffed marrow, with minced meat mixed with herbs; allow 1 tablespoonful of chopped Parsley, Thyme, Marjoram, a little Sage and a Bay leaf.

MUSHROOMS: Marjoram, Parsley, Tarragon.

ONIONS: Sage, Thyme.

PEAS: Basil, Mint, Rosemary, Tarragon, Chives, Savory. Any of these herbs may be boiled with the peas or sprinkled over them before serving.

POTATOES: Caraway, Chives, Dill, Marjoram, Mint, Parsley, Tarragon.

New Potatoes may be boiled with a sprig of any of these herbs, then rolled in butter and generously sprinkled with the chopped herbs.

Mashed Potatoes can have any of the herbs (chopped fine) added while beating.

Baked Potatoes—any of these herbs may be sprinkled on with the butter.

VINEGARS

HERB VINEGARS

Are easy to make and invaluable for providing various flavours for salads in their oil and vinegar dressings. They can also be used in stews, soups and rich gravies when 1 dessertspoonful of herb vinegar should be balanced by 1 level tablespoonful of jam.

MIXED HERB VINEGAR

To 4 pints of best white wine vinegar allow 2 oz. each of Balm, Chives, Shallots, Tarragon, Winter Savory and a handful of Mint. Pound these together to a pulp and put it into the vinegar. Cork tightly and keep in a sunny place for 2 or 3 weeks. Then strain, squeezing the herbs. Leave the vinegar to settle, then strain out the sediment through a cloth and bottle.

GARLIC VINEGAR

Skin and chop up about 2 oz. of Garlic cloves. Put them into a bottle with 1 quart of white wine vinegar, add a pinch of salt and cork. Leave 3 or 4 weeks, shaking the bottle occasionally, then strain and re-bottle.

SHALLOT VINEGAR

Cut up 10 Shallots and put them into a quart bottle of white wine vinegar. Cork and leave for a month, then strain and re-bottle ready for use.

TARRAGON VINEGAR

Gather the herb on a dry day in July before it flowers. Pick the leaves off the stalk and put about 4 oz. of them into a bottle, pour on a quart of white wine vinegar. Cork well and leave for 3 or 4 weeks before straining and re-bottling.

When supplies of this herb are limited, push a long spray of Tarragon into a pint bottle of white wine vinegar and leave it until the herb loses its colour, then remove it.

ELDER-FLOWER VINEGAR

Fill a jar loosely with the blossoms stripped from their stalks, cover them with white wine vinegar, cover the jar tightly and leave it for several weeks. Then strain and re-bottle ready for use.

VINEGARS IN VARIETY

Of Common Thyme, Lemon Thyme, Sage, Marjoram, Basil, Chervil, and Mint are made by placing a large bunch of bruised leaves of the particular herb in a bottle, covering them with white wine vinegar and leaving them to impregnate for several weeks before straining and re-bottling ready for use.

III. Scents—Toilet Uses

BATH SCENTS

Strong infusions of any fancied fragrant herbs are pleasant in the bath water. Lavender, Rosemary, Basil, Balm, Bergamot and Hyssop are old favourites.

ELDER-FLOWER WATER

As a complexion lotion, was once generally used and kept, like the toilet vinegars, in one of the lovely old-fashioned cut-glass bottles now found in antique shops. It is still effective as a mild astringent and tonic dabbed on the skin night and morning to clear and refine it. The infusion is especially good with a little borax and glycerine added, to use after sea-bathing.

To make Elder-flower Water, you fill a large jar with the flowers stripped from their stems, cover them with boiling water, and when slightly cooled, add (in proportion) ¾ of an ounce of rectified spirits to 1 quart of water. Cover with a folded cloth and keep in a warm place for several hours. When cold strain and bottle. Fresh or dried flowers may be used.

FOOT-BATH

Both soothing and refreshing, is made from Lavender leaves, fresh or dried, infused with boiling water.

HAIR-DARKENER

A strong infusion of Sage leaves applied to the scalp is said to darken the hair and invigorate its growth.

HAIR-WASH

Rosemary infused with a little borax added and used daily when cold is reputed to prevent dandruff and scurf.

HERB PILLOWS

Small pillows used to be stuffed with a mixture of dried herbs and scented flowers to place in beds, or they were placed under the head to induce sleep.

LAVENDER VINEGAR

Should be made to dab behind the ears and on the forehead; it is a very old and refreshing scent.

Fill a bottle very loosely with Lavender flowers and cover with white wine vinegar. Leave them to distil for 2 weeks in a sunny warm place, shake the bottle daily. After this time, empty the bottle and re-fill it with fresh flowers, cover them with the same vinegar strained. Repeat the process after another fortnight, making 3 infusions in all.

ROSE VINEGAR

A pleasurable relief for headaches after exposure to the hot sun, is made from either dried or fresh red Rose petals, steeped in white wine vinegar until it is thoroughly impregnated. The vinegar is then strained and bottled.

VIOLET VINEGAR

Another old favourite. To make it you fill a jar with Violet blossoms, cover them with white wine vinegar, cork tightly and leave in a warm place for 4 or 5 weeks, then strain and bottle.

VIOLET, JASMINE AND ROSE VINEGAR

A delightful old-fashioned scent and refresher is made by infusing 4 oz. of Rose petals and 1 oz. each of Violet, Lavender and Jasmine flowers in a bottle with enough white wine vinegar to cover them. Add ½ pint of Rose-water. The bottle is then closely covered and left in a sunny or warm place for 2 or 3 weeks, then the scented vinegar is strained and bottled.

SWEET BAGS

To lay among linens and clothing were made of muslin and filled with dried herbs such as Lavender, Rosemary, Hyssop, Marjoram, Bergamot, Basil, the ancient royal scent. Costmary, which keeps its balsam-like scent when dried, used to be mixed with Lavender for "Swete Bags," or made into bundles to lay on top of canopied beds, clothes-presses and wardrobes.

SWEET WASHING WATERS

These ancient skin-soothing luxuries can be enjoyed by half filling coarse muslin bags with the leaves of freshly-picked herbs or a teaspoonful of dried ones, and 2 tablespoonfuls of medium-ground oatmeal, then swishing and squeezing the bags into the water before washing or bathing· A bag may be used several times until the milky flow from the oatmeal is exhausted.

Balm, Basil, Bergamot, Rosemary, Lavender, Marjoram and Eau-de-Cologne Mint are delightful for Sweet water bags.

STINGS

The leaves of Basil or Savory rubbed on a bee or wasp sting give instant relief.

TEETH

Fresh Sage leaves rubbed on teeth clean and whiten them and strengthen the gums.

POT-POURRIS

Pot-pourris, the romantic sentimental old-fashioned mixtures of scented flowers, herbs and spices, can be made either *moist* or *dry*. The *moist* kind, which lasts for many years, is kept in china jars with lids that are often perforated, and is occasionally stirred to fill a room with its special summer scent. The *dry* sort is placed in open bowls, or put into muslin bags and sachets that have a number of pleasurable uses.

For either the *moist* or *dry* pot-pourris the bulk of the mixtures should be petals from very strongly-scented Roses, usually the red ones, particularly the Cabbage Rose and other old-fashioned types. Almost any other highly-scented flowers or leaves may be added. They should be gathered in the early afternoon when they are quite dry, not damped by dew or rain. They are further dried for the pot-pourris, spread out, and carefully separated on sheets of paper in an airy shaded room, as heat spoils the scent.

The herbs and flowers especially good in pot-pourris are the leaves of Bay, Balm, Basil, Bergamot, Costmary, Eau-de-Cologne Mint, Lavender, Myrtle, Marjoram, Rosemary, Santolina, Sweet Geranium, Verbena,

Rose petals, the flowers of Violets, Old Red Clove Carnations, Stocks, Jasmine, Orange and Lemon blossoms, Heliotrope, Lily of the Valley, Mignonette, Pinks, Lavender, Bergamot, "Mock Orange," Roman Chamomile.

The type and quantities of spices and other ingredients, in proportion to 2 gallons of petals, flowers and leaves, are: ½ oz. each of cinnamon stick, cloves, mace, Gum Benzoin, Gum Storax, allspice, Coriander seeds, powdered orris root or Violet powder, a few grains of musk. Sandalwood and cedar wood shavings help with their perfumes, and some recipes include thin strips of orange and lemon rind dried and pounded up with all the other spices.

With such a varied choice of ingredients it is possible to evolve a mixture that has a personal appeal.

For the *moist* preparation a mixture of roughly pounded salt is used, half common salt and half Bay salt (this is distilled from sea-water), about ½ lb. of each for a gallon jar of pot-pourri mixture. The petals and flowers and torn up leaves are only partly dried for this *moist* type, for about 2 days, then they are put into a glazed earthenware jar 2 handfuls at a time and firmly pressed down, a small handful of salt is sprinkled over them. Another layer of petals, etc., is added, sprinkled and pressed. The content of the jar is weighted down until the next supply of petals, etc., is ready. This process can be started quite early in summer and the jar can be filled up gradually as the flowers are available.

When completed, the mixture is taken out of the jar, broken up into small pieces and mixed with the powdered spices, aromatic barks, roots and the sweet powder. The freshly-made pot-pourri is then pressed tightly into a jar and left to mature for about 6 months. Should it get dry over the years, it may be moistened with a little brandy.

The *dry* pot-pourri has all the petals, flowers and leaves thoroughly dried, separated and spread out on papers in an airy room. They should be turned occasionally when drying. The spices, gums, etc., are pounded to powder, and when the whole mass is thoroughly mixed together it is ready for use.

To increase the pleasure of the dry pot-pourri, which is seen as well as smelt, some rosebuds and colourful flowers such as Larkspur, Delphiniums, Borage, Anchusa and Marigolds should be added.

IV. Growing Herbs in any Garden

IT is easy to accommodate a large variety of culinary herbs when a garden is available. In a tiny garden a small border in the sun can be devoted to the low-growing types and in a garden of any size the large ornamental kinds make excellent foliage plants to enhance flower borders. For instance, a beautifully-arranged bed at the base of a wall in the old Tilt yard at Dartington Hall shows the use of the tall fountains of Fennel's rich-green filmy foliage to contrast the pale green leaves and white silk blooms of Tree Poppies and Tree Peonies. And other herbs are admirably placed alongside large-flowered plants.

The gallant massive Lovage is often seen effectively used in herbaceous borders, as are groups of decorative Angelicas sometimes rising behind Delphiniums. Alecost makes an attractive clump of greyish-green leaves for pale contrast to bright flowers, and Tansy with its dense growth of dark-green foliage, like Prince of Wales' feathers, should be planted where it will be enjoyed but where its invasive roots may be checked. The smaller bushes of Hyssop and Rue, the lace-leaved Artemisias, with dusky Rosemary, grey Lavender and Sage can all be set to advantage in a thoughtfully-designed flower garden to complement such plants as Roses, Mallows, Phlox, Delphiniums, Lilies, etc. The varieties of Thyme with silver, golden, black or green, fragrant leaves, make evergreen cushions 2 feet across, at the front of borders or on flagstones, and the silvery-leaved Curry Plant and Santolina are good beside Carnations and Pinks. Dark-leaved Winter Savory forms a small evergreen bush providing it is in a dryish spot where the soil is not too rich. It must grow hard or it suffers in severe winters. A Sweet Bay that is allowed to develop naturally and is not pruned into formal shape, as it appears in tubs beside the doors of expensive restaurants, is an elegant tree that will grow in a partly shaded site.

MAKING A HERB GARDEN

To enjoy fully the pleasure of growing herbs and appreciating their scent and beauty, an enclosed secluded garden should be devoted to them. A mature herb garden is an enviable possession. Surrounded by a hedge or hurdles even a small piece of ground twenty feet square in a sunny position can be made extraordinarily attractive. Such little gardens should be as Pliny the Elder described those of ancient Rome, "daintie places of pleasure within the very citie."

A good lay-out to follow is the old formal plan of two intersecting paths at least three feet wide, forming a cross (to scare the devil), and when space permits with borders and paths around the surrounding wall, hedge or fence. Raised beds like those favoured by the early monks keep the soil well drained and save a lot of bending. These are easy to make if the paths are marked out and the top-soil is removed from them on to the beds. This method gives an added depth of good top-soil for the plants. The paths are thus sunken, and the beds should be supported by low walls of old bricks or stone which give ample opportunities for growing in the crevices fragrant-leaved creeping plants like Thymes and Mints. The paths may be paved and planted with carpeting Thymes and other creeping plants set between the flags or bricks. Or they may be gravelled so that a hoe will keep them free from weeds. Stone-paved or brick paths look lovely, but they are dangerously slippery in wet weather, whereas gravel is always safe and durable if it is spread on a firm foundation of stones and ashes, rolled hard when it is wet enough to be tightly compressed with a roller.

To enlarge the centre of the crossing paths, the corners of the beds may be either cut at an angle or rounded, to give space for a feature such as a sundial, a stone table, an antique urn or small statue. Another feature at the end of a path can be a low Thyme seat, as in the herb garden at Sissinghurst Castle. This should be made with largish stones set in soil with various Thymes planted between the stones so that they grow over and cover them with scented cushions.

In such a garden every plant has its particular use and beauty, the aromatic evergreen herbs and shrubs are heartening in winter, and during the rest of the year the foliage has the same rich and subtle tones as the herbage in an old tapestry, varying from greenish-silver through all shades of pale to dark green and gradations of purple and bronze.

The herbs are scented in leaf and bloom and there are the bright flowers of Bergamot, Poppies, Old Clove Carnations, Nasturtiums, Marigolds, strongly scented Roses, Anchusa, Borage, Comfrey, Violets, and the flat creamy umbels of Elder's blossoms, of Angelica's and Sweet Cicely's. And even the "purists" may plant Madonna Lilies, as they are ancient useful inhabitants of herb gardens; for many centuries their white petals were put in brandy or other pure spirit and kept in sealed jars to provide convenient antiseptic dressings for wounds.

TOWN HERB GARDENS

Town gardens can be made to produce a number of attractive culinary herbs, especially those with smooth leaves that do not hold grime as do the hairy-leaved ones. As the soil in many old town gardens is generally acid and sour and spoiled by cats and dogs, planting herbs should not be attempted until the ground has been cleaned and dug over incorporating some compost or humus material. This may be bought dry in convenient packages which are easy to handle and, if necessary, carry through the house. There are several good compounds available such as Seaweed Manure, Hop Manure, "Bac" Peat, Leaf-mould, etc. When the soil has been fed and a few days before planting, a dressing of Hydrated lime should be applied on the surface at the rate of about $\frac{1}{4}$ lb. per square yard. This will help to sweeten the old soil. And to make more certain of success, a hole should be dug 8 or 9 inches deep for each plant, a handful of manure should be placed at the bottom, then it may be filled up with John Innes Standard Potting Compost. If the plant is set in this reliable soil and watered in, it should be happy. Draughty sites must be avoided, and most herbs prefer as sunny a situation as possible.

Another idea for coping with a town garden is to build up artificial beds with side-supports of wood or old bricks, which are often obtainable from demolition sites. These beds may be made on any surface, concrete, asphalt, very bad ground or on a lead roof. Largish stones must be laid at the bottom and spaced so that water can drain away, on top of these should be placed a layer of old turves top downwards, then some small stones before it is filled up with good soil such as John Innes Standard Potting Compost. A border against a wall may be made in the same way and the soil should slope forward from the wall to allow rain-water to spread downwards.

Strong wooden boxes can also be used as plant containers. These should stand on a few bricks to facilitate drainage, and sufficient holes for draining must be made in the bottom, preferably with a red-hot poker, as this charring prevents rot. And to preserve the inside of the box, it is a good plan to burn paper in it just enough to char the surface. The outside should be painted and the filling is the same as for an artificial bed.

Window-boxes, tubs, half-barrels, troughs and large jars or urns, are all useful and ornamental plant containers for town dwellers, and they should all be filled with crocks for drainage, and John Innes Standard Potting Compost. Some lumps of charcoal mixed with the soil helps to keep it sweet for a long time.

Earthenware Strawberry jars, the large decorative ones with pocket-like holes on the outside to contain plants, make very attractive and useful containers for herbs and hold a useful variety. A barrel can be used in the same way with holes about 3 inches in diameter drilled and cut in the sides. When planting in such containers, put the drainage material at the bottom, then fill up with soil to the level of the first holes. Fold the plant's roots in tissue paper to prevent damaging them, and place them carefully through the hole, then from the inside remove the paper and spread the roots over the soil and cover up to the next holes. Repeat this planting process till the tub or jar is filled, then plant on top.

Plants in town gardens need not be choked with chemical-laden air if their foliage is regularly syringed with clean water.

SUITABLE HERBS FOR TOWN GARDENS

SHRUBBY PERMANENTS: Sweet Bay, Rosemary, Lavender (Nana compacta), Sage, Artemisias, Rue, Hyssop, Winter Savory, Roses, Thymes.

HERBACEOUS PERENNIALS: Marjoram, Tarragon, Fennel, Lemon Balm, Mints, Bergamot, Lovage, Chives.

BIENNIAL: Angelica.

ANNUALS FROM SEED: Borage, Chervil, Basil, Parsley.

HERBS FOR WINDOW-BOXES: Chives, Sage, Marjoram, Winter Savory, Tarragon, Parsley and Fennel can be grown if kept small by nipping off the growing points. Mint should be confined in a pot sunk in the box to keep its roots in check.

HERBS FOR POTS ON INDOOR WINDOW-SILLS.

Thymes, Chives, Marjoram and Mints are useful and reliable, but any of the small herbs such as Bush Basil should be tried.

The pots need to stand on gravel so that air may circulate and the roots do not become waterlogged; this may be contained in plant saucers that match the pots, or a zinc or other rust-proof tray, that fits the sill and holds a layer of gravel, will accommodate a number of pots.

John Innes Standard Potting Compost is ideal for pot plants and for any other purpose where perfect soil is required, but when buying this mixture it must be ascertained that it comes from a reliable source and that very coarse sand has been used in its blending.

DRYING HERBS FOR WINTER USE

Herbs are ready for drying and storing for use in winter just before they bloom when all the flavorous constituents are still in the foliage; later, much of them goes into the flowers. The sprays for drying should be cut in dry weather during the morning before the hot sun has affected their essential oils. Many types are ready in May and June, including Broad-leaved Sage, which does not bloom. Tarragon, Marjoram, Winter Savory, Lemon Thyme, Lemon Balm, Mint, follow in June and July, but Parsley's harvesting depends on when the seeds were sown.

Lavender flowers have their strongest scent just before the buds are fully open in late July and the first week in August. It is advisable to cut Lavender stems long enough to include a few leaves at the base. This light pruning of the plant helps to keep it shapely.

Aromatic herbs for pot-pourris are usually right for gathering in July and August.

It should be remembered that a plant suffers a set-back when it is cut too hard and greedily. But when sufficient foliage is left to supply its needs, and if, after the operation, it is given the restoring tonic of some nitrogenous fertilizer such as a sprinkling of dried blood or of sulphate of ammonia, lightly hand-forked and watered in to the soil around the plant, it will produce fresh growth. The cutting should act as a pruning to keep bushy plants neat and compact. If the evergreen types such as Thymes, Sage, Winter Savory, etc., are left uncut they invariably grow leggy.

DRYING HERBS FOR HOME USE

Is simple so long as only a few loose bunches are attempted at once. Two or three a day are coped with more easily than a large bundle which not only takes a long time to dry in the middle but loses its flavour, and often becomes musty inside.

The bunches should be loosely tied so that air may freely circulate through them, and hung up high in a dry warm airy room or shed, away from the sun which lessens their flavour. When the leaves are thoroughly dry and crisp they are ready to be rubbed into powder and stored in sealed jars in a dry dark place.

An alternative method of drying herbs that is convenient when the weather is wet and cold or misty is to hang the bunches from the bars on the top shelf of a very, very cool oven with the lower shelves removed.

Short Bibliography

Book of Sauces, The, by Ambrose Heath (London, 1948).
Cook's Guide, The, by C. E. Francatelli (London 1877).
Culinary and Salad Herbs, by E. Sinclair Rhode (London, 1940).
English Housekeeper, The, by Elizabeth Raffald (London, 1814).
English Physician and Complete Herbal, by Nicholas Culpepper (London, 1655).
Englishman's Flora, The, by Geoffrey Grigson (London, 1955).
Farmhouse Fare, "Farmers' Weekly" (London, 1940).
French Cooking for English Kitchens, by M. & L. Bonney (London, 1930).
French Dishes for English Tables, by J. Berjane (London, 1930).
Good Jams, Preserves and Pickles, by Ambrose Heath (London, 1947).
Herbal of All Sorts, by Geoffrey Grigson (London, 1959).
Herbs and the Fragrant Garden, by M. E. Brownlow (London, 1957).
Modern Herbal, by M. Grieve (London, 1931).
Plant Names Simplified, by A. T. Joynson and H. A. Smith (London, 1947).
Simple Salads, by Ambrose Heath (London, 1943).
Traditional Fare, by N.F.W.I. (London, 1948).

hERBS
and fRuit
foR slimmERS
CERES

This book explains how certain herbs can help to get rid of superfluous flesh and — if taken with various fruits such as grapefruit, avocado pears, tomatoes, peppers and mushrooms — can even help to prevent the formation of unwanted layers of fat. Moreover, slimming herbs can be taken in the form of teas or tisanes.

Herbal slimming entails losing weight slowly and regularly while living on a health-giving and high quality diet which includes the necessary balance of nutritious ingredients. This is far healthier and safer than embarking on crash diets, that often only consist of a weight-losing and weakening variety of foods which cannot satisfy and are therefore abandoned quickly.

The word 'herb' is taken to mean the buds, flowers, seeds, fruits, leaves, stems and roots of any traditionally tested and approved beneficial, remedial or culinary plant. Some of the commonest, like dandelions and cleavers, though regarded as weeds, are the most useful herbs of all.

herbs and fruit for vitamins

CERES

Most vitamin deficiencies take time to show up. They often become more obvious at periods of our development when body demands are higher, as in infancy, childhood, puberty, adolescence, pregnancy, during the menopause and in old age. Signs that the body is crying out for a supply of different vitamins also appear after prolonged bouts of anxiety or illness. Antibiotics, in the process of killing off harmful bacteria, often create a vitamin shortage, notably of vitamin B.

In this book the author provides valuable hints for adding vitamin-containing herbs, dormant and sprouting seeds, and fruit, to a diet which should be further enriched by organically-grown wholewheat bread; other whole grains, like brown rice; ripe, uncooked fruit (without sugar); fresh salad and green vegetables.

Scientists are on the verge of discovering many previously unsuspected plant virtues and in Britain, Europe, Russia and the U.S.A. they are discovering significant facts about the largely unrecognized values of common and uncommon herbs.

heRBS foR healthy haiR

CERES

Hereditary baldness is something that creeps up on many men and however much trouble they take to avoid the consequences, it seems impossible to overcome. Women, too, have their difficulties, as increasing numbers of them are suffering from premature greying of the hair.

But Ceres and other herbalists say that both processes can be halted! Or at least hindered! For example, there are many old recipes for remedying baldness and in this book readers will find prescriptions involving ingredients such as kelp, lemon, marigold, nettle, parsnip and rosemary. Dry and brittle hair can be benefitted by sunflower, almond or sesame oils and non-oily herbs like parsley, marigold and comfrey.

Every facet of hair-care is featured in these pages. The author provides remedies for alopecia, baldness, dandruff, dry and greasy hair, together with herbal recipes for hair colourers and conditioners, setting lotion, shampoos, rinses, hair oils, brushing lotions and stimulants for hair growth.

herbs
to help
you sleep
CERES

Modern orthodox medicine has little to offer the insomnia sufferer except harmful narcotics, most of which originate from the poisonous opium poppy. In the form of sleeping-pills these drugs have an anaesthetizing effect on the consciousness and brain, which may outlast the sleeping period – with possibly dangerous results. Furthermore, there are different levels of sleep, all of which have to be experienced for deep refreshment. Sleeping-pill sleep does not enable you to reach these levels – that is why it is not so refreshing.

But there are many harmless, health-giving, non habit-forming herbs and simples that can help you to sleep. Twenty of them are described and illustrated in this book. What keeps you awake? Chamomile may be taken for toothache, valerian and mullein for earache, alfalfa tincture for headache, Ignatia or 'St Ignatius Bean' for great sorrow and grief.

Not all the herbs mentioned have to be taken internally. Author explains the benefits of a hop pillow (George III gave one to his wife), and an ordinary pillowcase containing sprigs of rosemary and a bay-leaf.